CONTRIBUTION TO THE CRITIQUE OF THE CONCEPT OF UNDERDEVELOPMENT OF ECLAC

JOSÉ EULOGIO TORRES ÁBREGO

Ibukku is an auto-publishing company. The content of this work is the responsibility of the author and do not necessarily reflect the views of the publisher.

Published by Ibukku.
www.Ibukku.com
Graphic design: Índigo Estudio Gráfico
Copyright © 2017 José Eulogio Torres Ábrego
All rights reserved.
ISBN Paperback: 978-1-64086-016-2
ISBN eBook: 978-1-64086-017-9
Library of Congress Control Number: 2017953510

ÍNDICE

PROLOGUE

5

I. INTRODUCTION

9

II. CONTRIBUTIONS AND INSUFFICIENCIES OF THE
CONCEPTION OF UNDERDEVLOPMENT OF ECLAC

16

1. THE INDUSTRIAL REVOLUTION AS STARTING
POINT AND FIRST GREAT CONTRIBUTION OF ECLAC
AT THE SAME TIME THAT REVEALS OF ITS FIRST
GREAT WEAKNESS: ITS CONCEPTION OF THE
POLITICAL ECONOMY AS SCIENCE.

16

2. THE DEFICIENT TREATMENT OF THE "PERIOD OF
EXPANSION OR OUTWARD DEVELOPMENT" AS A
SECOND INSUFFICIENCY OF ITS CONCEPTION.

25

3. THE DENIAL OF THE IDEOLOGICAL CHARACTER
OF THE THOUGHT OF ECLAC AS ITS THIRD GREAT
INSUFFICIENCY.

28

4. THE THEORY OF "DEPENDENCE" AS ANOTHER
OF THE WEAKNESSES OF THE ECLAC CONCEPTION.

34

5. DIALECTICS AS THE APPROPRIATE METHOD
FOR THE TREATMENT OF THE ECLAC CONCEPTION.

47

III. THE SLOW SPREAD OF TECHNICAL PROGRESS IN
THE PERIPHERY AS A POINT OF DEPARTURE AND MAIN
WEAKNESS OF THE CONCEPTION OF
UNDERDEVELOPMENT OF ECLAC

55

1. THE CENTRAL AXIS OF THE THEORY
UNDERDEVELOPMENT OF PREBISCH-ECLAC

55

2. THE GREAT DEPRESSION OF 1929-30 AND THE
PREBISCH RUPTURE WITH THE NEOCLASSIC SCHOOL

70

3. THE CREATION OF ECLAC IN 1948 AND ITS
ATTEMPT TO ELIMINATE IT IN 1951

77

4. THE IMPULSE TO INDUSTRIALIZATION AND THE
IDEOLOGICAL ANTAGONISM THAT PLACES ECLAC
AND THE DEPARTMENT OF STATE IN THE ANTIPODE
OF THE CONTRADICTION.																85

IV. THE IMPORTANCE OF "STYLE", "MODEL" OR
"PERIOD OF EXPANSION OR OUTWARD DEVELOPMENT"
IN THE HISTORY OF UNDERDEVELOPMENT								92

1. THE DEFINITION OF THE "STYLE", "MODEL" OR
"PERIOD OF EXPANSION OR OUTWARD
DEVELOPMENT" AS A STRUCTURE, AS
RELATIONSHIPS OF PRODUCTION CONCERNING
THE "CENTRO-PERIPHERAL SYSTEM"									92

2. THE THEORETICAL-HISTORICAL PREMISES THAT
EXPLAIN THE APPEARANCE OF THE SOCIAL
CLASSES SPECIFIC TO UNDERDEVELOPMENT.						98

3. TOWARDS A PRECISION OF THE "OLIGARCHY"
CONCEPT IN LATIN AMERICA: FROM "MODERN
OLIGARCHY" TO "TRADITIONAL OLIGARCHY".						104

4. THE FAILURE OF THE BOLIVARIAN IDEAL: THE
VULCANIZATION OR FRAGMENTATION OF LATIN
AMERICA.																126

V. THE NATURE OF STATES IN LATIN AMERICA						155

1. A FALSE CONCEPTION OF THE STATE IN LATIN
AMERICA																155

2. THE NATION AND THE FORMATION OF THE
NATIONAL STATES IN EUROPE IN THE EIGHTEENTH
AND NINETEENTH CENTURIES. PARTICULARITY
IN THE CASE OF LATIN AMERICAN COUNTRIES					159

3. SOME WRONG VARIANTS ABOUT THE NATURE
OF THE STATE IN LATIN AMERICA.									177

4. WHY WAS THE UNITED STATES INDUSTRIALIZED
IN THE NINETEENTH CENTURY WHILE ARGENTINA
DID NOT ACHIEVE IT?													186

PROLOGUE

In this paper I present the results of my critical review of ECLAC's conception of underdevelopment. ECLAC is undoubtedly the most advanced school in the theory of underdevelopment. Emphasizing their fundamental contributions, which, in my opinion should serve as the basis for the development of a theory of underdevelopment, as well as the limitations and insufficiencies that have prevented a scientific conception, constitutes the purpose for this work. It contains five chapters.

In the introduction, we emphasize that the Industrial Revolution as a starting point for underdevelopment, as well as the recognition of the concepts of *underdevelopment and peripheral center* system make up significant contributions of this school.

In the second chapter, we emphasize that ECLAC's recognition of the Industrial Revolution as a starting point for underdevelopment is at the same time its first great weakness: its conception of Political Economy as a science, that is, as a relationship between things (Between *technical progress* and the *distribution* of productivity increases resulting from technological progress or technological change, for example) or between man and things, typical of the neoclassical school, and not as the study of relationships between men in the productive process; As well as the fragility of the ideological character of his thought, and the shallow depth of study and the analytical significance of the *style, model or period of expansion or outward development.*

In the third chapter, we focus attention on **Prebisch's main theoretical contribution and the starting point of**

Furtado's theory of underdevelopment, that is, in his conception of underdevelopment as a **structural rupture caused by the slow propagation of technical progress perpetuated by International division of labor;** Emphasizing that the division of the world economy into industrial centers on the one hand, and peripheral countries of primary production on the other, is not the product of the uneven propagation of technical progress, as Prebisch argues, **but the inexorable result of the new international division of labor that implanted the Industrial Revolution to unleash the process of integration of the world economy.** In other words, the **"center-periphery system"** is not the result of a structural rupture caused by the slow spread of technical progress and perpetuated by the international division of labor but, on the contrary, **the new international division of labor is the basis which explains the slow spread of technical progress in the periphery.** This conception of the underdevelopment of ECLAC constitutes its main weakness, that is to say, the true Achilles heel of all its theory.

In the Fourth chapter we deal with the insufficient treatment of the so-called *period, style or model of expansion or outward development,* in the evolution of ECLAC's underdevelopment theory, indicating that it is absent in the five stages or *synthesis table of the elements which compose ECLAC's thinking, according to Ricardo Bielschowsky,* which completely disrupts said table, since it eliminates the period of formation of the specific and responsible social classes of underdevelopment, that is, of the **modern oligarchy formed by the export-importing anti-national bourgeoisie that emerged after the Industrial Revolution, when the new international division of labor was introduced, as a direct result of the process of integration of the world economy.** This is the reason that has prevented ECLAC from elaborating a scientific theory of underdevelopment.

In the fifth and final chapter we defined, on the basis of the specific social classes responsible for underdevelopment, the nature of the States in Latin America, emphasizing that the States that emerged as a result of the independence process never established, organized and consolidated, as regional thinking has maintained, as national states. Conversely, they were always organized and consolidated as instruments of the Latin American oligarchies. Sometimes as an expression of the traditional oligarchy (the case of the Mexican state until the triumph of liberalism with Juarez, or of the Brazilian state of the Empire era); Others as a form of domination of the modern oligarchy (the Argentine state throughout the nineteenth century and practically until the triumph of radicalism); And not infrequently, as an instrument of the alliance between the modern oligarchy and the traditional oligarchy (the Mexican State of the Porfiriato or the Brazilian State of the First Republic).

Finally, it should be pointed out that, with this paper, we are laying the foundations, in our opinion, for the scientific elaboration of a theory of underdevelopment.

I express my gratitude to everyone who contributed to its preparation.

THE AUTHOR
Panama, January 2017.

I. INTRODUCTION

In the process of awareness of the objective reality arise certain concepts through which man fixate and express the proprieties, characteristics and links of the objects and phenomena's of the outside world. The concepts that reflect the most important aspects, links and or characteristics of a field of phenomena's constitute its **categories**. Each science possesses its own categories. In the case of the field of Theory of underdevelopment its categories arise during the first postwar period.

After the Second World War, in publications of the United Nations began the utilization of the category **underdeveloped** to designate the **specific-historical reality** of the peripheral countries linked to the capitalist system. It was expressed, with this category, the set of properties, characteristics, links and relationships, **generally-essential and specific**, of the new phenomena that reached in the process of its evolution the point of its full maturity. It was the way, to say it in a different manner, that the thought was taking ownership of this new historical reality. To such a point did society become aware of the underdevelopment that innumerable dependencies arose state, international, academically and university wide by those overseeing the phenomenon.

"If in 1944 -as stated by Cecilia Nahon, Corina Rodriguez Enriquez and Martin Schorr-, did not exist not even an international organism specially dedicated to this purpose [...], during that year and to this date more than forty international organisms of development of the underdeveloped were created, within and outside of the United Nations system. (More so) [...] one of the substantial contributions of the Latin American production of its time -the authors add- it was its role in the constitution of a novel field of study in the social sciences:

*the one here mentioned denominated **field of development of the underdeveloped** [1]*

It's not difficult to infer, therefore, that the significance of the emergence of the category of *underdevelopment* consists in that at that moment underdevelopment as a historical phenomenon culminates in its formation process, that is, it completes all of its fundamental phase phases to the point where society becomes fully aware of the fact and is preparing to study and confront it.

Seen in this way, underdevelopment lends itself as a **concrete totality**, as a set of characteristics, properties, links, determinations, relations, etc., that make up its content.

---

(1) Cecilia Nahón, Corina Rodríguez Enríquez y Martín Schorr, *El pensamiento latinoamericano en el campo del desarrollo del subdesarrollo: trayectoria, rupturas y continuidades [The Latin America way of thinking in the field of developmet of the underdeveloped: Trayectory, ruptures and continuations]*; pp. 330, 327-328; Tomado de [Taken from] **Crítica y teoría en el pensamiento social latinoamericano [Critisism and theory in the social thinking of Latin America]**; Buenos Aires: CLACSO, 2006, ISBN 987-1183-55-0; 448 pages. Entre la larga lista de organismos creados a partir de 1944 se destaca la fundación del Banco Internacional de Reconstrucción y Fomento [Among the long list of organizations created since 1944, highlights the foundation of the International Bank for Reconstruction and Developmant] (1944), Fondo Monetario Internacional [International Monetary Fund] (1944), Fondo de las Naciones Unidas para la Infancia [United Nations Fund for Children] (1946), Banco Interamericano de Desarrollo [Inter-American Bank for Development] (1959), Organización para la Cooperación y el Desarrollo Económico [Organization for Cooperation and Economic Development] (1960), Banco Africano de Desarrollo [Bank of Africa for Development] (1963), Instituto de Investigación del Comercio y el Desarrollo [Institute for Research in Trade and Development] (1964), Banco Asiático de Desarrollo [Bank of Asia for Developmient] (1965), Programa de las Naciones Unidas para el Desarrollo Social [United Nations Program for Social Development] (1963), Conferencia de las Naciones Unidas para Naciones Unidas para el Desarrollo [Conference of the United Nations for United Nations Development] (1965), etc. (Ibíd., p. 330-331).

Now, in the course of the historical process of knowledge categories do not all arise together and at the same time. Each of them is closely linked to a certain stage of the development of knowledge. By setting the relationships and properties that are manifested in that particular stage, the categories reflect the particularities of that stage and appear as a step further in the stairway of knowledge, as a moment of transition from a lower stage to a higher one of the knowledge of the object by man.

In the case of ECLAC'S theory of underdevelopment, the appearance and emergence of its fundamental concepts and categories can be summarized as follows. Everything suggests, according to Octavio Rodriguez, that the concepts *center and periphery* were first used in 1946. From this concepts are emerging others as the so-called *outward development* in which new techniques are only implemented in the *primary-export sectors* to produce *food and raw materials at low cost* to large *industrial centers*. A relationship arises in which *the terms of trade* imply that *the purchasing power of industrial goods of an export unit of primary goods* decreases with the passage of time. The tendency to inequality between *the two poles* of the *center-periphery system* is inherent to its dynamics and characteristic of the *outward development* phase. The *demand for industrial imports* from the centers tends to grow relatively quickly, while their *primary exports* tend to grow relatively slowly. Hence the tendency to the *external strangulation* inherent in the periphery of the *industrialization* proper to the *period of inward expansion* that begins *spontaneously* with the First World War and continues with The Great Depression of the thirties and the Second World War. After a period of boom in the process of industrialization in the fifties and sixties, a process of *internationalization of the internal market* and of *economic stagnation* is reached. There is the synthesis.

It is evident; therefore, that concepts and categories, besides **reflecting** the phenomena's properties, links, etc., are at the same time points of support and reflect **different degrees** in the development of knowledge, that is, different moments of transition from lower stages to higher stages of object knowledge. Hence the reciprocal-natural link and dependence between concepts and categories, the need to conceive them as steps of the same stairway of knowledge, as a solid and logical system in which each category occupies its **place and only its corresponding place**.

It should be emphasized, however, that the *underdevelopment* category the cornerstone of underdevelopment theory has not been widely accepted in the field of political Economy.

Shortly after its appearance, the organisms of Nations replaced the category *underdevelopment* by the concept (países en desarrollo) **developing countries**. Authors such as Bettelheim and a number of scholars of the dependency theory questioned, in turn, the validity of the category.

*"Personally," says Bettelheim, "I think that if the problems of the most destitute people are designated by the expression problems of **underdevelopment countries** and not by some scientifically more accurate expression, this is due to the conscious and unconscious effort, of bourgeois ideology. From a scientific point of view, he adds, it is necessary in my opinion to substitute the expression "underdeveloped countries" for the more exact expression of **exploited, dominated countries** with a deformed economy" [2]. "The **dependency** concept," says Theotonio Dos Santos "emerges in Latin America as a result of the process of discussion on the subject of underdevelopment and*

---

(2) Charles Bettelheim, **Planification et croissance aceélereé [Aerial Planning and Growth]**; Francois Maspero; pp. 26-27; París, 1967. Negritas de José E. Torres A. (JETA)

*development. To the extent that the expectations of the effects of industrialization are not fulfilled, the development theory that underlies the national and independent development model elaborated in the 1950's is called into question; the overcoming of previous errors is that of **dependence**"* [3].

Not all representatives of the so-called *dependency theory* accept, nonetheless, this point of view. Thus, for some authors, the concept of dependence expresses a specific feature of underdevelopment rather than a category that substitutes the latter.

"Dependence," Silva Michelena and Heinz Rudodolf, "is a specific and inescapable trait of underdevelopment; This dependence has a structural character, that is to say, that it forms part of the set of relationships of production that form the basis of the socio-economic formation called underdevelopment" [4].

Nevertheless, the great majority of the authors of this "school" accepted the first position, that is to say, to the extent that the theories on industrialization advocated by the ECLAC found no answer in Latin America reality, the concept dependence had to replace the concept of underdevelopment.

Well, these positions seem to us unfortunate.

---

(3) Theotonio Dos Santos, **Imperialismo y dependencia [Imperialism and dependence]**. Ediciones ERA, 1a. ed.; p. 300, México, 1978. Esta posición ya la había expresado Dos Santos en su trabajo [This position had already been expressed by Dos Santos in his work], *La crisis de la teoría del desarrollo y las relaciones de dependencia en América Latina [The Crisis of Development Relations in Latin America]*, que aparece en [that appears in] **La dependencia político-económica de América Latina [The polititcal-economic dependence of Latin America]**; Siglo XXI, 2a. ed., p. 173; México, 1970.

(4) Héctor Silva Michelena y Heinz Rudolf Sanntag, **Universidad, dependencia y revolución [University, dependence and revolution]**; Siglo XXI; 3a. ed., p. 89; México, 1973.

The lack of correspondence between the **specific, general and essential** characteristics of a phenomenon and the concept or category that designates it may justify the substitution of one concept for another, or when a concept because of its greater precision and accuracy is more adequate than another to refer to a particular relationship or objective process. But this is not the case. When the natural relation between the objective world and the categories is broken by an arbitrary management, the specific nature of the phenomena fixed in them is distorted. This is what happens with the concept of **dependency**. This category is not specific to the phenomenon; it does not arise with the development of that one. It is for this reason that when Cardoso affirms that[...] "Even without going back to periods before the twentieth century, in Lenin and Trotsky, for example, the expression dependence appears with some frequency" [5], does not realize that he is the victim of his own trap, because the connotation of this category reveals how different its content is, not only from the reality expressed by the concept of underdevelopment, but from that to which the students of dependence refer. Thus, when Lenin speaks of "the need to constantly explain and denounce before the broader working masses of all countries, and particularly of the backward countries, the deception systematically carried out by the imperialist powers, which, in the guise of politically independent states, create states that are totally dependent on them in the economic, financial and military sense" [6], does not refer to states that are totally dependent in the sense of a "relationship" of "unequal exchange" or of an "import substitution process"

---

(5) Fernando Henrique Cardoso, *Notas sobre el estado actual de los estudios sobre dependencia [Notes on the current status of studies on dependece]*, en **Desarrollo latinoamericano** [in **Latin American Development**] (ensayos críticos [critical tests]); selección de [selection of] José Serra; Fondo de Cultura Económico [Economic Culture Fund]; 1a. ed., p. 325; México, 1974.

(6) V. I. Lenin, **Obras Completas [Complete works,** Ed. Cartago, Tomo XXXIII, 292; Buenos Aires; citado por [quoted by] Vania Bambirra, **Teoría de la dependencia [Theory of dependency]: una anticritica [An anticritic];** Ediciones ERA [ERA Editions], 1a., p. 51 ; México, 1978.

frustrated and less than the "internationalization of the internal market", to cite just a few examples, since these **characteristic, particular and essential** processes of underdevelopment (dependence) were not known at the time. In addition, Lenin never used the category dependency to designate as it does with the category imperialism, to a phenomenon or specific totality; to speak of totally dependent states (or countries) does not mean, in any way, to speak of dependence (underdevelopment) in the sense of a historically concrete material formation. It is no coincidence, therefore, that there is, as Cardoso points out[...] "A gap of half a century between the current wave of analysis of dependence in the Latin American bibliography and the formulations of the classics of Marxism".[7]

Hence the need to use the category of ***underdevelopment*** instead of *dependence* to refer to the historical-specific reality of countries on the periphery of the capitalist system. It is a new category to designate a new phenomenon which represents a great progress in the conceptualization of the fundamental problem of contemporary economic science.

Maintaining the use of the category of **underdevelopment** despite attempts by the current dependency in ECLAC to replace it with the concept of *dependence* in the late 1960s is one of the main merits of Prebisch.

"We have presented," says Prebisch, "our concept of dependency relations to prevent confusions that are not infrequent. ***The so-called underdevelopment is thus attributed to dependence. It's confusing dependency and underdevelopment".***[8]

---

(7) Fernando Henrique Cardoso, Ob. cit. pp. 325-326

(8) Raúl Prebisch, **Capitalismo periférico [Peripheral capitalism]. Crisis y transformación [Crisis and transformation],** Fondo de Cultura Económica

II. CONTRIBUTIONS AND INSUFFICIENCIES OF THE CONCEPTION OF UNDERDEVLOPMENT OF ECLAC

1. THE INDUSTRIAL REVOLUTION AS STARTING POINT AND FIRST GREAT CONTRIBUTION OF ECLAC AT THE SAME TIME THAT REVEALS OF ITS FIRST GREAT WEAKNESS: ITS CONCEPTION OF THE POLITICAL ECONOMY AS SCIENCE.

Of course, the phenomenon and the category that designates it are two completely different things. Underdevelopment as a historical-natural phenomenon arises with the Industrial Revolution, while its category appears after World War II when the phenomenon culminates its gestation. In recognition of the Industrial Revolution as a starting point for the underdevelopment, I think it is ECLAC's first contribution to the development of a scientific theory of underdevelopment, at the same time as its first great weakness: the conception of economics as a science.

"In the long period from the Industrial Revolution to the First World War, new forms of production in which technology has been unceasingly manifested only a small proportion of the world's population. The movement begins in Great Britain, continues with varying degrees of intensity in the

---

[Fund of Economic Culture], primera edición [first edition], p. 206; México, D. F., 1981.) (Negritas del JETA [JETA Bold])

European continent, acquires an extraordinary impulse in the United States, and finally encompasses Japan, when this country is determined to assimilate quickly the Western ways of producing. Thus formed the great industrial centers of the world, around which the periphery of the new system, vast and heterogeneous, played a small part in the improvement of productivity. Within this periphery, technical progress only engages in small sectors of its large population, since it generally does not penetrate but where it is necessary to produce food and raw materials at low cost, destined to those large industrial centers".[1]

"In the formulation of my point of view, emphasizes Prebisch, I mentioned from the beginning the role of technical progress. Among the main aspects of this phenomenon, my interest was attracted in particular by the international diffusion of technical progress and the distribution of its benefits, since the empirical data revealed a considerable inequality between the producers and exporters of manufactured goods, on the one hand, and producers and exporters of primary goods, on the other[...] The type of connection between each peripheral country and the center, and the extent of this connection, depended largely on its resources or on its economic capacity to mobilize them. In my opinion, this fact had the greatest im-

---

(1) Raúl Prebisch, *Crecimiento, desequilibrio y disparidades [Growth, imbalance and disparities]: interpretación del proceso de desarrollo económico [Interpretation of the Economic Development process]* (Primera parte del *Estudio Económico de la América Latina, 1949*, CEPAL [First part of the *Economic survey of Latin America*, 1949, ECLAC]); tomado de la Lectura N° 46* [Taken from Reading No. 46*], **La obra de Prebisch en la CEPAL [Prebisch's work at ECLAC],** Selección de Adolfo Gurrieri en dos partes [Selection of Adolfo Gurrieri in two parts], de la serie Lecturas de El Trimestre Económico [Of the Series of the Economic Quarter]; Fondo de Cultura Económica [Fund of Economic Culture], primera edición [first edition]; Primera parte [first part] (El programa inicial en la CEPAL [The initial program in ECLAC), p. 156; México, 1982.

portance, since it conditioned the economic structure and the dynamism of each country [...] [2]

In these statements that constitute the cornerstone of ECLAC's conception of underdevelopment, both its structuralism vision and its neo-structuralism vision reveal its first great weakness: its conception of economics as the study of relationships between things (between *technical progress* and the *distribution* of increases in productivity derived from technical progress or technological change, for example) or between man and things, typical of the neoclassical school. In the texts of Economic theory, whatever its origin and following Samuelson, Political Economy or Economics is defined as the study of:

"1) [...] activities that, with or without money, involve exchange transactions between people"; 2) [...] "the way in which people decide to use scarce or limited productive resources (land, labor, capital goods such as machinery and know-how) to produce various commodities (such as wheat, beef, coats , Yachts; concerts, roads, bombers) and distribute these goods among the members of society for consumption"; 3) [...] "people in their daily occupations to make a living and enjoy it"; 4) [...] "the way in which human beings organize their consumption and production activities"; 5) [...] "wealth"; 6) [...] "ways of improving society and making humanitarian civilization possible" [...] Today, adds Samuelson, economists agree on a general definition of the following: Economics is the study of the way in which people and society

---

(2) Raúl Prebisch, *Cinco etapas de mi pensamiento sobre el desarrollo [five stages of thinking about development]* (ensayo presentado en un seminario del Banco Mundial [Essay presented at a World Bank seminar]), en CEPAL [in ECLAC], **Raúl Prebisch: un aporte al estudio de su pensamiento [a contribution to the study of his thinking]**, LC/G.1461, p. 14-15; Santiago de Chile, marzo de 1987 [March 1987]. Publicación de las Naciones Unidas, N° de venta [United Nations publications, Sales No.] S.87.II.G.6.

end up 'choosing', using or not money, the use of 'small' productive resources that could have alternative uses to produce various 'goods and distribute' them for consumption, present or future, between different people and groups of society. The economy analyzes the 'costs and benefits' derived from the improvement of resource utilization patterns ".[3]

This conception of the Economy or Political Economy as relationships between things or between things and the man is a characteristic common to neoclassic and cepalistas and to which Prebisch could not give up when taking off the neoclassical thought.

"I believed," he points out, "in all that the classic books of the great centers had taught me. He believed in free trade and the automatic functioning of the gold standard. He believed that all development problems were solved by the free play of the forces of the international economy or of the domestic economy. But when the great world depression came, those years of anxiety led me to dismantle step by step everything I had been taught and throw it overboard. The contradiction between reality and the theoretical interpretation elaborated in the great centers was so great that interpretation was not only ineffective when it was put into practice, but also counterproductive ".[4] "I have done," he adds elsewhere, "a great an effort to escape these theories and to explain with intellectual independence the phenomena of peripheral development [...] As I once remembered, during my youth these theories se-

---

(3) Paul A. Samuelson, **Economía**, Libros McGraw Hill de México [**Economy, Books McGraw Hill of Mexico**], S.A., undécima edición [eleventh edition], p. 2; México, D. F. 1984.

(4) Raúl Prebisch, **Hacia una dinámica del desarrollo latinoamericano [Towards a dynamics of Latin American development]**, Fondo de Cultura Económica [Fund of Economic Culture], Primera reimpresión [First reprint], p. xii; México, D.F., 1971.

duced me by their precision and mathematical elegance; and also by its persuasive force".[5]

The neoclassical inheritance of this conception of economics as a relationship between things or things and man, as well as his "mathematical elegance", is so rooted in ECLAC that despite its truthful and forceful criticism of neoclassical thought, it remains unscathed and immovable until today. Nevertheless, Political Economy as a science has nothing to do with such a conception.

"Economics," Engels points out, "is not about things, but about relationships between people and, ultimately, between classes; while these relationships are always linked to things and appear as things. Although, some economist had already glimpsed this connection in isolated cases, it was Marx who discovered it in terms of its scope for the whole economy, thereby simplifying and clarifying the most difficult problems to such an extent which today even the bourgeois economists themselves can understand".[6] *"Political Economy," reaffirms Lenin, on the other hand, "is not concerned with **production** at all, but with the social relationships of men in production, and with the social system of production. Once these social relationships have been clarified and analyzed to the end, **with it**, the place of each class in production and, con-*

---

(5) Raúl Prebisch, **Capitalismo periférico [Peripheral capitalism]. Crisis y transformación [Crisis and transformation]**, Fondo de Cultura Económica [Fund of Economic Culture], primera edición [first edition]; p. 247; México, D. F., 1981.

(6) F. Engels, La Contribución a la crítica de la Economía política [The Contribution to the Critique of Political Economy], de Carlos Marx [From Carlos Marx]; **Obras escogidas [Selected Works]**; Editorial Progreso [Editorial Progress], Tomo I [Volume I]; p. 352; Moscú [Moscow], 1955.

sequently, the part of the national consumption that it receives is also determined".[7]

Since, Economics as a science, only deals with the social relationships of men in production, that is, dealing with the **social movement, with the higher and more complex form of the movement of matter, it is completely arbitrary and meaningless to pretend to mathematize it.**

*"The richer in determinations – and therefore in relationships – are the thoughts," Pythagoras points out, "**more intricate, on the one hand, and on the other more arbitrary and meaningless, becomes its representation in forms such as numbers".***[8]

This is the reason why Marx with full knowledge of the mathematics of his time, with more than 1,000 sheets in mathematics, never intended to apply mathematics to social sciences particularly to political economy. The application of mathematics to the sciences is only possible if it is a question of lower or simple forms of matter. But it is impossible in the biological movement or in the movement of human beings; and much less in the social relationships of men.

Here, as Engels transcribes it:

---

(7) V. I. Lenin, El desarrollo del capitalismo en Rusia [The development of capitalism in Russia] (el proceso de la formación de un mercado interior para la gran industria [The process of forming an internal market for the large industry); en **Obras completes** [In **complete Works**], Editorial Cartago, Tomo III [Volume III], p. 54; Buenos Aires, 1957.

(8) V.I. Lenin, **Cuadernos filosóficos [Philosophical notebooks] (la dialéctica de Hegel [Hegel's dialectic]);** Colección R, N° 46 [Collection R, No. 46]; Ediciones Roca [Roca Editions], S.A., primera edición [first edition], p. 40; México, D.F., 1974. Negritas de JETA [JETA Bold]

"Application of mathematics: in the mechanics of solid bodies, in an absolute way; in the case of gases, in an approximate way; in that of liquids, and more difficult; n physics, rather by trial and error; in chemistry, simple first-degree equations of the simplest character; in biology = 0 ".[9]

A similar point of view is found in Francisco Miro Quesada.

*"If we analyze the completely spontaneous and naive interpretation that neoclassical economists make of the general equilibrium formulas– he argues in his reflections on economic theory – we find the following situation. Variables are replaced by numerical constants denoting prices, quantities of goods, services, work, and so on. But no individual constant is associated with real individuals who are related to each other in such a way that prices, goods, work, and so on result from this relationship. That is, there is no room for agents who, ultimately, constitute the universe of the structure of interpretation (model). The functional terms (functions in the usual mathematical sense) that are used to elaborate the general equilibrium equations apply only to objects that result from the action of the human beings that make up the universe. And these objects come to be properties or relationships like prices and concrete objects that do not intervene in economic activity but are the result of it. **Individuals, sustenance of all properties and relationships and creators of all economic objects, are not part of the model. But this makes it impossible to form an adequate model, because it does not make sense to include properties and relationships (attributes) or***

---

(9) F. Engels, *Dialéctica de la naturaleza [Dialectic of nature];* en **Obras Fundamentales de Marx y Engels [In Fundamental Works of Marx and Engels]**, Colección dirigida por Wenceslao Roces [Collection directed by Wenceslao Roces], Tomo 18 [Volume 18] (F. Engels, Obras filosóficos [Philosophical Works]), p. 490; Fondo de Cultura Económica [Fund of Economic Culture], primera edición [first edition]; México, D.F., 1986.

constructed objects in the universe, if we do not include the individuals that are related, that have the properties and that construct the objects. [...] .. In essence, the main element of the universe of the structure is always the individual. *The universe can have, besides individuals, properties and relationships, in which case the connotation must have properties and relationships of second order or higher orders.* ***But without individuals the model cannot even begin to elaborate. And it is precisely the individuals, the real men of flesh and bone, the ultimate substrate of all economic and social activity, who are not included in the implicit model of general equilibrium theory [...].. so that the indicated equations can be interpreted unequivocally and rigorously it is therefore imperative to include individuals in the universe of interpretation. But once this is done, things get complicated, once individuals are considered the problem arises of reworking the functional terms so that they can refer to it. And when this reprocessing is done it is certain that relationships between the action of individuals, prices, goods and services can no longer be described by equations of equilibrium of the Walras-Paretian type. This seems to explain why the classical equations have no clear econometric meaning. They cannot have it, because, due to the lack indicated, they cannot express the relationships between the behavior of real individuals and the real economic consequences"***.[10]

This conception of the Economy as a relationship between things or between things and man is the first basic insufficiency of the school of ECLAC, its true Achilles heel, since it

---

(10) Francisco Miró Quesada, *Reflexiones sobre el concepto de teoría económica [Reflections on the concept of economic theory]*, en Serie de Lecturas de El Trimestre económico [In Economic Trimester Series of Readings], **Lectura N° 26 [Reading No. 26], Metodología y crítica económica [Methodology and economic critique]**; Selección de [Selection of] Camilo Dagum; Fondo de Cultura Económica [Fund of Economic Culture], primera edición en español [First edition in Spanish], p. 152; México, 1978. Negritas de JETA [JETA Bold]

ignores the nature of the specific social classes of underdevelopment, which I have called the *modern oligarchy* (the export-importing bourgeoisie) antinational and foreign, and underdevelopment is attributed to a simple relationship between *things*, between *technical progress* and the *distribution* of productivity increases, deriving from that technological progress or technological change. That is the crux of the matter.

It is important to underline that in some authors of ECLAC this weakness of their conception finds full recognition.

"The main limitation," says Octavio Rodríguez, "is that, by concentrating the analysis on the transformation of the productive structure, **ECLAC's thought leaves aside (or only examines, the sides and surface) the relationships between different classes and social groups, Which are the ones that ultimately drive the above transformation".**[11]

"Rightly so," says Prebisch himself in the Prologue to ECLAC's Theory of Underdevelopment, Octavio Rodriguez highlights in his book the limitations of **ECLAC's** *theories. They are strictly economic theories, with some circumstantial incursion into other fields. In ECLAC, sociologists and economists have been mismatched for a long time, thinking with some suspicion who dared to enter the fence that corresponded to the other. Well, I have made a modest essay on which I am still working. I am trying; in short, to interpret*

---

(11) Octavio Rodríguez, *La teoría del subdesarrollo de la CEPAL [The theory of underdevelopment of ECLAC]. Síntesis y crítica [Synthesis and criticism]*; en Serie de Lecturas de El Trimestre económico [In Economic Trimester Series of Readings], Lectura N° 40 [Reading No 40], **El análisis estructural en economía [Structural analysis in Economics]: ensayos de América Latina y España [Essays from Latin America and Spain]**; Selección de [Selection of] José Molero; Fondo de Cultura Económica [Fund of Economic Culture] /Instituto de Cooperación Iberoamericana [Institute of Ibero-American Cooperation], primera edición [First edition] , 1981 (España [Spain]), primera edición [First edition], p. 63; 1982 (México).

*peripheral development as a complex dynamic phenomenon that encompasses technical, economic, social, political and cultural elements. All this goes beyond the scope of economic theory, and I expose myself to the indifference of economists and the nonconformity of sociologists[...]. Whatever it may be, he adds later, this new theoretical adventure of mine, side executive responsibilities-represents **another phase in the development of ECLAC thought** and, as such, cannot escape our original concept of what has been termed a 'center-periphery scheme'"*.[12]

Unfortunately, in his attempt to renew his thinking, that is to say, in his neo-structuralist version his mature work *Peripheral capitalism* does not represent, from the point of view of the **specificity** of peripheral capitalism, no substantive progress with respect to the contributions of its first three works.

It is important to emphasize here, however, that in spite of the remnants that ECLAC theory could not overcome from the neoclassical, the most profound and compelling criticism against the neoclassical school comes from ECLAC, specifically from Prebisch. This is one of his great contributions and support. The independence of the thought of the region, as well as the absolute freedom of thought, so often defended and maintained by Prebisch, are principles that any Latin American thinker, no matter what his ideology, must pay taxes to ECLAC.

2. THE DEFICIENT TREATMENT OF THE "PERIOD OF EXPANSION OR OUTWARD DE-

---

(12) Raúl Prebisch, *Prólogo* a la obra de [*Prologue* to the work of] Octavio Rodríguez, **La teoría del subdesarrollo de la CEPAL [The theory of underdevelopment of ECLAC]**, Siglo xxi editores [21st Century publishers], octava edición [Eighth edition], p. x-xi; México, 1993

VELOPMENT" AS A SECOND INSUFFICIEN-CY OF ITS CONCEPTION.

The second shortcoming of ECLAC's theory of under-development is the poor treatment of the so-called *period of expansion* or *outward development* in ECLAC's history of thought. Moreover, in the **summary table of the analytical elements that compose ECLAC's thinking**, this fundamental period in the history of underdevelopment is absent.

"It can be identified", says Ricardo Bielschowsky, five stages in the work of ECLAC, around 'ideas-force' or 'messages'. By coincidence, each stage lasted approximately a decade. (A) Origins and the fifties: industrialization, (b) the sixties: 'reforms to unclog industrialization', (c) the seventies: a reorientation of the 'styles' of development toward social homogenization and towards export diversification, d) the eighties: overcoming the problem of external indebtedness through 'adjustment with growth', e) the 1990's: productive transformation with equity". [13]

As we can see, in the *summary table of the elements that make up ECLAC's thinking*, the *period of expansion or outward development* is absent, which completely disrupts this picture, since it eliminates one of the most important periods in the history of the phenomenon. In the process of historical evolution of underdevelopment three fundamental phases or periods are distinguished: **1)** *the period, style or model of expansion or outward development*, ranging from the Industrial

---

(13) Ricardo Bielschowsky, *Cincuenta años del pensamiento de la CEPAL [Fifty years of ECLAC thinking]: una reseña [a review]*; en **Cincuenta años de pensamiento en la CEPAL [In Fifty years of thinking in ECLAC] (Textos seleccionados [Selected texts]), volumen I [Volume I];** Fondo de Cultura Económica [Fund of Economic Culture] /CEPAL [ECLAC], primera edición [first edition], p. 12; Chile, 1998.

Revolution to the process of integration of the world economy and the new international division of labor, until the beginning of the *process of import substitution* that began with the First World War for the most advanced countries of the region, Argentina, Brazil and Mexico, with the Great Depression of 1929-30 for the middle countries, and with the Second World War for small countries, particularly Central America and the Caribbean; **2)** *the period, style* or *model of expansion* or *inward development* or *of import substitution*, which extended until the middle of the seventies with the process of *denationalization of industrial bourgeoisie*; **3)** *the period of transnationalization of the internal market* or *denationalisation of the Latin American industrial bourgeoisie* to the present day.

Of course, the five stages of ECLAC's work which are no more than the stages of its thought must therefore include the three stages or periods of the history of underdevelopment, not only because ECLAC and specifically Prebisch incorporate them, but because each of these periods is conditional on each other and form an indissoluble unity. Hence the contradiction in the *table-synthesis of the analytical elements that makes up the thinking of ECLAC.* The elimination of the *period, style or model of expansion or outward development* interrupts the history of its economic, social and political structures and deforms the reality of the phenomenon, that is, violates the very nature of the *historical-structural method.* This period represents to be the most important one, from the point of view of the formation of the specific social classes of underdevelopment, more than a hundred years of intense class struggle in the history of the region that are eliminated by a stroke. It is like trying to build the foundations of underdevelopment theory starting at the middle of the building. These inadequacies have prevented ECLAC from knowing, **First**, the specific social classes of underdevelopment, that is, of the *modern oligarchy (of the importing bourgeoisie and the* *export bourgeoisie), anti-national and foreign;* **Second**, of the class struggle between the modern oligarchy and the *traditional oligarchy (the great large estate)*, between *liberals and conservatives;* **Third**, of the intense class struggle between the modern oligarchy and the *nineteenth-century manufactory*, especially between Buenos Aires and the Interior, or, in other words, the failure of the Bolivarian ideology; **Fourth**, of the *nature* of the States that emerged and established themselves from the independence process; **And, fifth**; The impact of the new international division of labor imposed by the Industrial Revolution and the process of import substitution.

3. THE DENIAL OF THE IDEOLOGICAL CHARACTER OF THE THOUGHT OF ECLAC AS ITS THIRD GREAT INSUFFICIENCY.

The denial of the ideological character of ECLAC's thinking constitutes its third great insufficiency.

For some authors of ECLAC, the ideological character of their thinking is a fundamental characteristic of the institution and has a marked nuance in the region. What I find to be just and right.

*"At first glance," says Octavio Rodríguez, "ECLAC's contributions to economic theory seem designed to delineate the peculiarities of the spontaneous process of industrialization of the periphery and the transformations in the productive structure that accompany it, and the contributions of economic policy, to raise the policies by which it is possible and desirable to conduct that process in a deliberate manner. **Beyond this semblance of neutrality, the project that underlies such thinking reveals its ideological character, by making***

visible its links with the points of view and interests of particular groups and social classes.

The aforementioned project, as well as the thinking under study, which contains it, gives high priority to the interests of the national industrial bourgeoisie and, therefore; is compatible and convergent with them. It also has a polyclassist stamp, as it seeks to safeguard the interests of the middle classes, the workers and, in general, the vast dispossessed groups, based on the economic absorption and social integration that they are supposed to achieve with deliberate industrialization. According to all indications, it focuses on social relations from a specific perspective, broadly coincident with that of states linked to the state apparatus; Advocates the expansion of its functions and the degree of its intervention, and postulates that it is able to reconcile the interests of different groups and classes and privilege those of the nation as a whole. *It was previously said that ECLAC thought does not take social relations into account, or only examines them laterally and superficially. It is now possible to state, with greater accuracy, that this limitation is linked to the ideological character of that thought, because if it does not cover social relations, this is because it implicitly establishes with respect to them assumptions of ideological stamp [...] , Although the thinking of ECLAC significantly alters the assumptions of the conventional economy, providing a sui generis interpretation of underdevelopment, does not exceed the framework of that economy, which ultimately is circumscribed.*

"The socio-political project implicit in the contributions of the first decade," reiterates the author again, "can be compared to the populist ideologies that were in force in several Latin American countries during that decade and in the preceding two. The ECLAC project are similar to those of these ideologies, although they present their own in a

more explicit and extreme way, for example, they emphasize the contrast of national interests with those of foreign capital, and those of developed countries with which traditionally close economic ties have been maintained, and they recognize and emphasize the existence of confrontation and conflict between the social groups that make up the populist alliances, broadly in line with the beneficiary groups of the ECLAC project, and the groups opposed to them, linked to the large estate and the commercial and financial interests of the old primary exporting scheme. *Not only the implicit project, but also the own thinking of ECLAC of the fifties, is compatible and convergent with the ideologies mentioned. In other words, both these and that seem to form part of the same general movement of ideas, marked by a clear progressive tendency. Both propose economic and social changes that, although they presuppose the consolidation of the most dynamic groups of the capitalist class, also pretend the gradual economic absorption and social integration of the vast groups belonging to the dispossessed classes. It is also observed that in those years the proposed changes present visibility of viability, because with different nuances and degrees of success, depending on the cases, several alliances of populist power try to put them into practice ".*[14]

The same point of view is found in Ricardo Bielschowsky and in Celso Furtado.

"It should be noted," says Bielschowsky, "that Brazil was probably the country of the region in which the foundational ideas of ECLAC had a wider acceptance [...]" The concept that predominated throughout the period was that of developmentalism, whose main elements Are: the valuation of industrialization as a way to development, and the importance of the role of the State in planning, financing and investment

---

(14) Octavio Rodríguez, Ob. Cit. pp. 98-100. Negritas de JETA [JETA Bold].

*in those sectors in which private initiative is insufficient. It is pointed out that although developmentalism would no longer be the organizing theme of the economic debate in the 1960s, the developmental state would be prolonged much more in time[...]To understand this evolution, the key concept is the **ideological cycle of developmentalism**, According to which developmental thinking originated between the 1930s and the end of the Second World War, matured over the next ten years, lived its boom during the government of President Kubitschek (1956-1960), and made crisis in the early years of the 1960s[...]"The most important of the ECLAC theoretical contribution to the Brazilian debate was to have given developmental economists what might be called a new analytical system: the theory of peripheral development".[15]*

"In Brazil in the 1940s and early 1950s," Furtado added, "the debate was about whether or not to privilege the country's industrialization policy. Translated into current terms: what would be the best way to promote development? Adopt an industrial policy or entrust everything to the market? Both at that time and today, the answer to that question is no stranger to the definition of the social forces that guide strategic economic decisions. In the years to which I refer, the dominant social forces in Brazil were linked to rural interests and foreign trade. I remember that as an ECLAC technician I participated in a meeting of Latin American entrepreneurs that took place in Santos in late 1949. The central theme of the debate was the cost of industrialization experienced by the countries of the region during the world conflict. The prevailing view was that it was appropriate to return to the classical form of development, which relied on the comparative advantages of interna-

---

(15) Ricardo Bielschowsky, **Ideología y desarrollo [Ideology and development]: Brasil, 1930-1964**; en Revista de la CEPAL [In ECLAC Magazine], N° 45, pp. 155-156; Santiago de Chile, diciembre de [December] 1991. Negritas de JETA [JETA Bold].

*tional trade. That was the universally accepted good doctrine. During my speech, I discreetly referred to the desirability of exploring opportunities for industrialization. In fact, the model of an 'essentially agricultural' economy advocated by the Brazilian ruling class had begun to be questioned since the 1930s. I was one of the first to denounce agrarianism as the cause of our backwardness. A country of Brazil's expansion and heterogeneity could not depend on extensive agriculture to develop. Today that seems elementary, but half a century ago was a hotly contested controversy. The truth is that more than 90% of Brazilian exports were agricultural primary products, and interests linked to foreign trade were those that occupied the command positions in the country. It was not that the country was totally lacking in industries. Already there was the matrix of an industrial nucleus whose representation was circumscribed to certain areas. **What there was not was an industrial system capable of generating its dynamism. The pace of economic activity was directed from the outside and, therefore, by the primary activities. The problem was not limited to the fact that in order to grow it depended on the importation of technology and equipment, but had to have a ruling class capable of formulating a project to transform the country. The modernization project of the country would have to rely on these forces. When I was convinced that the rising industrial class could take on that historical role, I set to work to forge the tools it needed to play it"*.[16]

Strangely, Raul Prebisch's position on the ideological character of ECLAC's thinking does not coincide with the point of view of these authors; moreover, it is completely contrary.

---

(16) Celso Furtado, **En busca de un nuevo modelo [Looking for a new model] (Reflexiones sobre la crisis contemporánea [Reflections on the contemporary crisis]);** Fondo de Cultura Económica [Fund of Economic Culture], primera edición en español First edition in Spanish]; pp. 90-92 Buenos Aires, Argentina, 2003. Negritas de JETA [JETA Bold].

"I do not agree with him," says Raúl Prebisch in the **Prologue** to Octavio Rodríguez's book, *"The Underdevelopment Theory of ECLAC,"* **when he argues that in the early writings of the CEPAL, a certain ideology linked to new interests arises with the development of industrialization. I say 'new interests', because from our writings there are no manifestations of approval to the prevailing regime of land tenure. I do not share that doctrinal suspicion of our friend.** *It is true that industrialization is done by men and that it enables many of them to thrive more than would be due to their efforts because of the abusive protection they have been given. But this does not mean that, in advocating industrialization, our design has been the prosperity of those. Prosperity has come in addition. And if Octavio Rodríguez remembers that work of 1953, he will see that there is sought to increase the accumulation and to accelerate the rate of growth at the expense of that frankly exaggerated prosperity.* **So you might ask:**

Who ultimately favors ECLAC ideas? I admit that the answer was not absolutely diaphanous in its day. I think mine is now without a doubt. And that the ideological bias is completely different than that assumed by the author of this volume. *In any case, the ideological character of my writings has always been and will continue to be debatable. And we must accept this reality, which, by the way, does not stop offering certain stimuli.* **But the populist bias that Octavio Rodríguez also discovers is very different. This surprises me, for among the many epithets I have been pointed out in my long existence I do not remember the populist voice. Populism sometimes has a profound significance. It is the expression of human feelings and aspirations that are generally unknown to the favored strata of the social structure. Populism, however, is characterized by flattering these feelings and aspirations without trying to penetrate deep into the serious social problems. Nothing is stranger to the temperament of**

Octavio Rodríguez, who has great human sensitivity. And that also sinks deep, in reality. I could not be a beloved advisor to a populist ideologist!". [17]

It should be emphasized that the ideological character of ECLAC's thinking does not invalidate the scientific character of its positions, since the latter is determined by the interests of the specific classes in question. Thus, for example, the interests of the industrialization process advocated by ECLAC and, therefore, the national bourgeoisie of the underdeveloped countries coincide with the interests of the development of society. Hence, its revolutionary character. Conversely, the interests defended by large landowners are contrary to the interests of the development of society and consequently its reactionary character. The ideology of a social class ceases to be scientific when its interests as a class no longer correspond to the interests of the development of society, that is, when its ideology ceases to be revolutionary to become reactionary.

4. THE THEORY OF "DEPENDENCE" AS ANOTHER OF THE WEAKNESSES OF THE ECLAC CONCEPTION.

Among the fundamental inadequacies of the theory of underdevelopment of ECLAC, the dependency theory, specifically the version of Fernando Henrique Cardoso and Enzo Faletto,

---

(17) Raúl Prebisch, *Prólogo* a la obra de [Prologue to the work of] Octavio Rodríguez, **La teoría del subdesarrollo de la CEPAL [The theory of underdevelopment of ECLAC]**, Siglo xxi editores [21st century publishers], octava edición [Eighth edition], pp. xii-xiii; México, 1993. Negritas de JETA [JETA Bold].

Dependence and Development in Latin America, deserves special attention because of the great contrariety and its profound theoretical repercussion, which summarizes and expresses the thoughts of the authors who subscribe.

Let us see, then, the crux of the matter.

*"Towards the mid-1960s," says Cardoso, "within and outside the ECLAC began to develop another line of interpretation - more sociological and political - that, although it did not immediately incorporate itself into the thought of the institution, would later appear in the Texts by Vuskovic, Celso Furtado, Osvaldo Sunkel and others. This line came to be known as **the theory of dependence"**.* [18]

To the extent that the theories on industrialization advocated by ECLAC found no answer in Latin American reality, the concept of dependence, as Theotonio Dos Santos points out, had to replace the concept of underdevelopment. [19]

"When that picture was already on the horizon, in the mid-1960s," Cardoso adds the so-called "dependency approach" gained strength as a "counter theory" or "against ideology" that simultaneously criticized ECLAC formulations

---

(18) Fernando Henrique Cardoso, **La originalidad de la copia [The originality of the copy]: la CEPAL y la idea de desarrollo [ECLAC and the idea of development]**, en Revista de la CEPAL [In ECLAC Magazine], N° 4, p. 206; Segundo semestre de 1977 [Second half of 1977].

(19) Theotonio Dos Santos, **Imperialismo y dependencia [Imperialism and dependence]**, Ediciones ERA [ERA Editions], 1a. ed.; p. 300, México, 1978. Esta posición ya la había expresado Dos Santos en su trabajo *La crisis de la teoría del desarrollo y las relaciones de dependencia en América Latina* [This position had already been expressed by Dos Santos in his work *The crisis of development theory and dependency relationships in Latin America*], que aparece en **La dependencia político-económica de América Latina** [Which appears in **The Political-Economic Dependence of Latin America**]; Siglo XXI [21st century], 2a. ed., p.17; México, 1970.

and those of the traditional left. The latter continued to see in the alliance "large estate imperialism" the great enemy of development.

"The notions of underdevelopment and development - Cardoso finally asserts - lead to a very different appreciation, since according to them the developed economies have a structural conformation different from that which characterizes the underdeveloped ones, since the structure of the latter is, to a significant degree, a result of the relationships that existed historically and still exist between both groups of countries. **The notion of dependence, (which, it should be repeated, was disseminated in Santiago by sociological criticism), is already incorporated into the approach, although in a version closer to the opposition between dominant and dominated countries".** [20]

This **theory of dependence** and in spite of what Octavio Rodríguez claims [21] did not incorporate, despite its good intentions, the class analysis to the study of dependence.

---

(20) Fernando Henrique Cardoso, *El desarrollo en capilla* [*The development in chapel*] (*Este texto fue escrito en 1979 para el ILET de México* [*This text was written in 1979 for the ILET of Mexico*]); en Serie de Lecturas de El Trimestre económico [In Economic Trimester Series of Readings], Lectura N° 40 [Reading No 40], **El análisis estructural en economía [Structural analysis in economics]: ensayos de América Latina y España [Essays from Latin America and Spain]**; Selección de [Selection of] José Molero; Fondo de Cultura Económica [Fund of Economic Culture] / Instituto de Cooperación Iberoamericana [Institute of Ibero-American Cooperation], primera edición [first edition], pp. 38,33-34; 1981 (España [Spain]), primera edición [first edition], 1982 (México). Negritas de JETA [JETA Bold].

(21) "En paralelo al tipo de análisis de fuerte arraigo económico[...]..-identificable como *enfoque CEPAL -Prebisch-* existen otros de base definidamente sociológica, en los que se inscriben las contribuciones de Medina Echavarría, de clara raíz weberiana[...]..En más de un sentido, la versión del *enfoque* de *la dependencia* debida a Cardoso y Faletto resulta complementaria de las dos recién mencionadas. Y ello en tanto esa versión encara los procesos de desarrollo de la región desde el ángulo de las estructuras políticas. A través de la revisión de

"More than anything," Villamil points out, "this new approach to development problems has led to a greater emphasis on the study of changes in the world economic system. In particular, greater importance is attached to the growing hegemony of transnational corporations and the implications of this situation". [22]

---

múltiples experiencias históricas, sus autores brindan sustento a la hipótesis de que la conformación de una hegemonía política, así como de las bases del poder político que definen su fisonomía -las cuales, en condiciones de dependencia propias de la periferia, combinan grupos e intereses nacionales y foráneos- abren distintas opciones de transformación, tanto en el propio ámbito político, como en los ámbitos social y económico que están en su base ["Parallel to the type of analysis of strong economic roots [...] ..- identifiable as *ECLAC -Prebisch approach-* there are others with a definite sociological basis, in which are inscribed the contributions of Medina Echavarría, of clear Weberian root [...] In more a sense, the version of *the dependency approach* due to Cardoso and Faletto is complementary to the two mentioned above, and this as it approaches the development processes of the region from the angle of political structures. The authors support the hypothesis that the conformation of a political hegemony, as well as the bases of political power that define its physiognomy - which, in conditions of dependence of the periphery, combine groups and interests National and foreign - open up different options for transformation, both within the political sphere itself and in the social and economic spheres that are at the root of it]. (Octavio Rodríguez, **El estructuralismo latinoamericano [Latin America structuralism]**, Siglo XXI [21st century] / CEPAL [ECLAC], primera edición [first edition]; p. 17; México, 2006).

(22) J.J. Villamil, *Introducción* [*Introduction*], en Serie de Lecturas del El Trimestre económico [In Economic Trimester Series of Readings], **Lectura N° 37 [Reading No. 37], Capitalismo transnacional y desarrollo nacional [Transnational Capitalism and National Development]**, José J. Villamil (compilador [compiler]); Fondo de Cultura Económica primera edición en español [Fund of Economic Culture first edition in Spanish], corregida y aumentada [Corrected and increased], p. 11; México, 1981. Villamil se refiere aquí al artículo de Sunkel [Villamil refers here to Sunkel's article], *Capitalismo transnacional y desintegración nacional en la América Latina [Transnational Capitalism and National Disintegration in Latin America]*, **Estudios internacionales [International Studies]**, núm. 4 [no. 4], enero-marzo de 1971 [January-March 1971]. **"El enfoque de la dependencia –sostiene Villamil- no es una teoría; al contrario y como ha señalado Fagen se trata más bien de un "marco conceptual, de un conjunto de conceptos, [...]de una óptica que pretende ubicar y aclarar una amplia gama de problemas ["The dependency approach," Villamil maintains, "is not a theory; on the contrary, and as Fagen has pointed out, it is**

However, this **theory of dependence** headed by Cardoso and Faletto profoundly disrupts the foundations of Prebisch-ECLAC's conception of underdevelopment.

"We have presented," says Prebisch, "our concept of dependency relationships to prevent confusions that are not infrequent. ***The so-called underdevelopment is thus attributed to dependence. It is to confuse dependence and underdevelopment.*** *At the periphery, both the phenomena of dependence and the exclusionary and conflicting tendencies that characterize underdevelopment are presented. As it was said elsewhere, if the former disappeared by art of enchantment, those tendencies would subsist. On the contrary, if the dynamics of capitalism were as it were imagined, and transnational corporations would invest and reinvest indefinitely in the periphery,*

---

rather a" conceptual framework, a set of concepts, [...] an approach that seeks to locate and clarify a wide range of problems"]". (R. Fagen, *Studying Latin American Politics: Some Implications of a Dependencia [Dependence] Approach*, **Latin American Research Review**, Vol. XII, núm. 2 [no. 2]; citado por Ibíd [Cited by Ibid].) "Es una manera de enmarcar los problemas del desarrollo poniendo hincapié en el estudio del sistema capitalista global y de las relaciones entre los países del centro y de la periferia de éste. Parte del supuesto de que la historia de los países de la periferia y la de los países del centro no son historias paralelas, sino que más bien son la misma historia. El desarrollo de la América Latina en el siglo actual está relacionado con su evolución histórica, con su pasado colonial y con el desarrollo del capitalismo en sus distintas fases. El subdesarrollo comienza a entenderse como una condición que no surge única ni primordialmente de deficiencias nacionales inherentes a las ociedades subdesarrolladas, sino más bien de la forma como estos países se han incorporado al sistema capitalista mundial ["It is a way of framing the problems of development with an emphasis on the study of the global capitalist system and the relations between the countries of the center and the periphery of the center. Part of the assumption that the history of the countries of the periphery and of the countries of the center are not parallel histories, but rather they are the same history. The development of Latin America in the present century is related to its historical evolution, its colonial past and the development of capitalism in its different phases. Underdevelopment begins to be understood as a condition that does not arise solely or primarily from the national deficiencies inherent in the underdeveloped voices, but rather from the way in which these countries have been incorporated into the world capitalist system"]". (Ibíd. p. 11). Negritas de JETA [JETA Bold].

the system's absorbing capacity would be accentuated and underdevelopment would be progressively eliminated. This would lead to this paradoxical conclusion: the greater the dependence, the greater the social efficiency of the system! But the system does not work like that. And the transnationals do not pursue the goal of achieving this social efficiency, but of collecting sooner or later the harvest of their investments. We said a moment ago that it is attributed to dependence, however interpreted, the responsibility of underdevelopment. Translated into our language, it means that the poverty of the masses excluded from development would have been created by the action of the centers. Nothing is gained in the field of theory, as well as in that of praxis, with this kind of statements, which does not mean denying them efficiency in political in-doctrination". [23]

From the above, it is not difficult to reveal the profound contradictions between the theory of dependence and the conception of Prebisch-ECLA underdevelopment, but also the contradictions within the theory of dependence itself.

All Latin American scholars, Marxists or non-Marxists, have a fundamental premise: "underdevelopment is not a backward and pre-capitalist stage but a consequence of it and a particular form of development". At this point there is no disagreement in the region. The divergences begin when it comes to defining which phase of capitalism corresponds to underdevelopment.

---

(23) Raúl Prebisch, **Capitalismo periférico [Peripheral capitalism]. Crisis y transformación [Crisis and transformation],** Fondo de Cultura Económica [Crisis and transformation, Fund of Economic Culture], primera edición [first edition], pp. 206-207; México, D. F., 1981.) Negritas del JETA [JETA Bold].

Not a few scholars of the *theory of dependence* believe in the sixteenth century to discover the origins of underdevelopment.

"The colonial period", as the example given by Silva Michelena and Heinz Rudolf "is the period of the emergence of underdevelopment and its structural pendency [...]. It can still be seen at this point that the roots of underdevelopment are not simply the roots of backwardness. The simple delay, they add, existed until the fifteenth century, before European expansion, before this time there was no underdevelopment, which is a product of capitalism".[24] "Once the capitalist contradictions of polarization and expropriation - appropriation of the surplus at the international internal level - pointed in the same direction by Frank - have been introduced in Latin America, their necessary consequences, namely: a limited development or underdevelopment in the metropolis Of the continent and the development of structural underdevelopment, far from delaying its appearance several centuries, until after the Industrial Revolution in England as it is suggested so many times, began to generate and emerge immediately [...] Latin America - continued - began its life And its post-conquest history as an integral and exploited part of world capitalist development, and this is why it is still underdeveloped today"[25] [...] "Unlike most independent societies within present-day capitalism, according to the same line, Anibal Quijano, the historical-social formations that gave rise to the present national societies of the region were constituted as ab Initio, as part of the process of formation and development of the capitalist

---

(24) Héctor Silva Michelena y Heinz Rudolf Sanntag, **Universidad [University], dependencia y revolución [Dependence and revolution]**; Siglo XXI [21st century]; 3ª. Ed.; p. 79; México, 1973.

(25) Andre Gunder Frank, *Chile: el desarrollo del subdesarrollo [The development of underdevelopment]*, en [in] **Monthly Review —Selecciones en Castellano [Selections in Spanish]** - número doble [Double number]; pp. 31, 34; enero-febrero [January-February]; 1968.

system of dependence, in its colonial period [...] ..The colonialist dependence gave way to imperialist dependence.The first gave rise to the historical formations of Latin American colonial capitalism; secondly, their constitution as dependent national societies within the industrial capitalist system" [26]. *"In any case," added Cardoso and Faletto, "the situation of underdevelopment occurred historically when the expansion of commercial capitalism and then industrial capitalism linked to the same market economies that, in addition to presenting different degrees of differentiation of the productive system, to occupy different positions in the global structure of the capitalist system"* [27].

This approach seems completely wrong. As a product of capitalism, underdevelopment could not arise in an age (the primitive accumulation) in which capital had not conquered the domestic market, let alone the world market. The integration of the world economy and the emergence of underdevelopment correspond to a higher phase of the evolution of capitalism, to the period of the Industrial Revolution and the great machined industry. Post-conquest history (the phase of commercial capitalism) could not therefore begin the process of integration of Latin America into world capitalist development, for at that time capital existed primarily under the embryonic form of commercial-usurer capital and As such had not deprived feudalism of the sphere of production.

---

(26) Aníbal Quijano, *Dependencia y cambio social [Dependence and social change]*, en **América Latina [in Latin America]: dependencia y subdesarrollo [Dependence and underdevelopment]**; EDUCA [EDUCATE], 1ª ed., pp. 108-109; Centroamérica [Central America], 1973.

(27) Fernando Henrique Cardoso y Enzo Faletto, **Dependencia y desarrollo en América Latina [Dependence and development in Latin America] (ensayo de interpretación sociológica [Sociological interpretation essay])**; Siglo XXI [21st century], 6a. ed., p. 23; México, 1972.

At this point we agree with ECLAC and the authors who in one way or another are linked to this school (Sunkel, Furtado, etc.). However, there are some dependents who locate the origin of underdevelopment in the Industrial Revolution. This is the case of Octavio Ianni and Ruy Mauro Marini.

"In the economic perspective, structural dependence," Ianni- indicates "is the product and condition of the internationalization of the productive process. It is born with the 'international division of labor' generalized by the expansion of industrial capitalism".[28] "It is from that moment on," says Marini "that Latin American relations with European capitalist centers are inserted in a definite structure: the international division of labor, which will determine the course of the further development of the region. In other words, It is from then on that the dependence is formed, understood as a relation of subordination between formally independent nations, in which the relations of production of subordinate nations are modified or recreated to ensure the extended reproduction of dependence".[29]

As we see, in the central point of the **origin of dependence** (underdevelopment), there is no agreement between the authors of the so-called *dependency theory*.

In our view, the position of Silva Michelena, Rudolf Sanntag, Andre Gunder Frank, Aníbal Quijano, Cardoso and Faletto and others, does not represent any progress on what Prebisch-ECLAC had already put forward, that is, the thesis

---

(28) Octavio Ianni, *La dependencia estructural [Structural dependence]*, en **América Latina [in Latin America]: dependencia y subdesarrollo [Dependence and underdevelopment]**; EDUCA [EDUCATE], 1ª ed., p. 118; Centroamérica [Central America], 1973.

(29) Ruy Mauro Marini, **Dialéctica de la dependencia [Dialectics of dependence]**; Ediciones ERA [ERA Editions]; 3a. ed., p. 18; México, 1977.

of the **Industrial Revolution as a starting point for under-development.** Contrarily it means a setback.

This is not, on the other hand, the only weakness of dependency theory. Most of their representatives consider that **the theory of dependence is inseparable from the theory of imperialism.**

[...] "The concepts imperialism-dependence," states Lanni, for example, "are twin complementary concepts (pairs), reciprocally necessary and determined, one produces the other, and the two are produced and reproduced in the other, they correspond to two poles Complementary, diverse, antagonistic and dialectical of the capitalist system considered as a whole". [30] *"In other words, structural dependence reveals, in detail, the way in which imperialism is inserted and diffused within the subordinate society, or how the internalization of imperialist relations, by the dependent society".* [31]

The same opinion is found in Cardoso. In his controversy with Weffort [32] on the problem of dependency, Cardoso stresses:

---

(30) Octavio Ianni, Ob. cit., p. 141.

(31) Octavio Ianni, **Imperialismo y cultura de la violencia en América Latina [Imperialism and culture of violence in Latin America]**; Siglo XXI [21st century], 2a. ed., p. 12, México, 1971.

(32) Véase los trabajos de [See the works of] Francisco C. Weffort, *Notas sobre la teoría de la dependencia ¿Teoría de clase o ideología nacional?* ; Y Fernando Henrique Cardoso, ¿Teoría de la dependencia o análisis concreto de situaciones de dependencia? [*Notes on Dependency Theory Class theory or national ideology?* And Fernando Henrique Cardoso, *Theory of dependence or concrete analysis of situations of dependence?*]; publicados bajo el título [Published under the tittle], *Dos opiniones sobre el problema de la dependencia [Two opinions on the problem f dependence]*, en la revista **Comercio Exterior** [In the **Foreign Trade** magazine]; abril de 1972 [April 1972].

[...] "I do not agree with the simplistic way Weffort solves the confrontation between dependence theory and imperialism theory. There is no theory of dependence independent of imperialism theory. The confrontation is artificial"[33] [...] "It is essential," says dos Santos, on the other hand, "in the current state of the debate, linking the study of dependence to that of imperialism and the international economy that generates".[34]

This position does not seem right either.

The concepts imperialism-dependence are not, as these authors claim, complementary concepts, reciprocally necessary and determined. While there is a relationship between underdevelopment (dependence) and imperialism, it is nevertheless true that this relationship is never expressed as an organic link. These phenomena are born and develop independently of each other. We have already seen that underdevelopment arises as a consequence of the new international division of labor implanted by the Industrial Revolution as the world economy is integrated. Its development corresponds, therefore, to 21st century. Conversely, imperialism is a phenomenon of the late nineteenth and early twentieth centuries and its appearance has no direct, internal or necessary relationship to underdevelopment (dependence). It is evident; therefore, that those phenomena (underdevelopment -dependence- and imperialism) and the concepts in which they are expressed are not reciprocally necessary and determined one therefore does not produce the other.

---

(33) Ibíd., p. 363.

(34) Theotonio Dos Santos, Ob. cit., p. 366.

These remarkable errors inevitably lead to their authors, and hence to the whole theory of dependence, to profound, insurmountable, and insoluble contradictions.

It cannot be maintained as Octavio Ianni does [...] that **"structural dependence** is the product and condition of the internationalization of the productive process. **It is born with the 'international division of labor' generalized by the expansion of industrial capitalism"**; to later affirm that [...] **"the concepts imperialism-dependence are twin complementary concepts, (pairs), reciprocally necessary and determined. One produces the other; and the two are produced and reproduced in each other"**; or as Fernando H. Cardoso does when he emphasizes that **"there is no theory of dependence independently of the theory of imperialism. The confrontation is artificial"**; and then to affirm with Enzo Faletto that [...] **"the situation of underdevelopment occurred historically when the expansion of commercial capitalism and then industrial capitalism** linked to the same market economies that, in addition to presenting varying degrees of differentiation of the productive system, came to occupy different positions in the global structure of the capitalist system", or that **"dependence compatible with the formation of national producers, is therefore prior to the development of capital-exporting monopoly imperialism"**.[35]

As we can see, the contradictions are obvious.

The contradictions that arise from the notable errors of the *so-called theory of dependence* inevitably lead to the collapse of the foundations that serve as the foundation; Hence, the ste-

____

(35) Fernando Henrique Cardoso, ¿Teoría de la dependencia o análisis concreto de situaciones *de dependencia [Theory of dependency or concrete analysis of situations of dependency]?* en Ob. Cit., pp. 364-365. Negritas de JETA.

rility of the theory to bear fruit and the justification of Gerard Pierre's reproaches.

"Based on the general theoretical approach to the particular mode of structural relationships inherent to dependency", says this author, "one could expect to arrive at the concrete study of these structural relationships. However, this level of concreteness is at best deficient in the theoretical treatment and analysis of the dependency of the majority of scholars. It is true that at that point 'dependents' are dedicated to the description of structures. [...] However, rather than indications and descriptions, it is necessary to reach the middle of the dynamics of these societies and their articulation to the center". [36]

The frustrated attempt of Marini, who proposed an ambitious theory to explain the "dialectic of dependence" by the necessary super-exploitation of labor in the periphery (source for it, of unequal exchange), was overthrown by the critics of Serra and Cardoso. [37]

Putting things that way, it is pretentious to say that [...] *"the theory of* dependence must be understood as the creative

---

(36) Gérard Pierre Charles, *Teoría de la dependencia, teoría del imperialismo y conocimiento de la realidad social latinoamericana [Theory of dependence, theory of imperialism and knowledge of Latin American social reality]*, en **Economía Política [Political Economy]**, publicación del Instituto de Investigaciones Económicas y Sociales de la Universidad Nacional Autónoma de Honduras [Publication of the Institute of Economic and Social Research of the National Autonomous University of Honduras], No. 12, p. 73, mayo-octubre de [May-October] 1976.

(37) Véase José Serra y Fernando H. Cardoso, *Las desventuras de la dialéctica [The misadventures of dialectics]*, y, Ruy Mauro Marini, *Las razones del neodesarrollismo* [The reason for New Development] (Respuesta a [Answer to] F. H. Cardoso y J. Serra), en Revista mexicana de sociología [in Mexican Journal of Sociology], número extraordinario [Extraordinary number]; enero [January], 1978.

application of Marxism-Leninism to the understanding of the specificities assumed by the laws of movement of the capitalist mode of production in countries such as Latin America" [...].[38]

5. DIALECTICS AS THE APPROPRIATE METHOD FOR THE TREATMENT OF THE ECLAC CONCEPTION.

Finally, we have to define what method we have to deal with underdevelopment theory, particularly the ECLAC-Prebisch school theory, which is undoubtedly the most advanced of the schools of underdevelopment that exist today.

We have already said that underdevelopment as a *historical phenomenon* and the *category* that designates it are two completely different things. Underdevelopment as a **historical-natural phenomenon subject to objective laws that do not depend on the will of men** arises with the Industrial Revolution, while its category appears after the Second World War. Categories or concepts only appear when the phenomena expressed in them have matured enough to give birth to them. Underdevelopment, therefore, reaches its full maturity after World War II; it is in this period that the **phenomenon completes all the phases of its historical formation**, where it presents itself as a *concrete totality*, as a *unit of the diverse, synthesis of many determinations*. The *underdevelopment category* is the form, as the thought appropriates this new historical reality and prepares to study it. This explains why this

---

(38) Vania Bambirra, **Teoría de la dependencia [Theory of dependence]: una anticrítica [An anti-criticism]**; Ediciones ERA [ERA Editions], 1ª ed [1st edition]., p. 26; México, 1976.

is the starting point of the research. Hence the certainty of Marx's assertion.

"The concrete is concrete, because it is the synthesis of many determinations, that is, unity of the diverse. That is why the concrete appears in thought as the process of synthesis, as a result, not as a starting point, even if it is the true point of departure and, therefore, the starting point also of perception and representation". [39]

The materialistic character of Marx's dialectic should be emphasized here.

"My dialectical method is not only on its basis other than Hegel's method, but is directly its reverse. For Hegel, the process of thought, which he even converts, under the name of idea, into a subject with life of his own, is the demiurge (creator) of the real, and the real its simple external form. For me, on the contrary, the ideal is nothing more than the material transposed and translated in the head of man [...] **The mystification undergone by the dialectic in the hands of Hegel**, *he points out later,* **does not detract from the fact that he was the first to expose, in all its amplitude and with all consciousness the general forms of its movement. In Hegel the dialectics goes upside down. It is necessary to put it on its feet to discover the rational grain covered under the mystical crust"**. [40]

---

(39) Carlos Marx, **Contribución a la crítica de la economía política** [**Contribution to the Critique of Political Economy**], Ediciones de Cultura popular [Popular culture editions], S.A. 6ª ed., p. 258-259; México D.F. 1974.

(40) C.Marx, *De las palabras finales a la segunda edición alemana del primer tomo de El CAPITAL [From the final words to the second German edition of the first volume of El CAPITAL]*, en **Obras escogidas en dos tomos** de [in **Works selected in two volumes** of] C. Marx y F. Engels; Editorial Progreso [Editorial Progress], Tomo I [Volume I]; p. 434; Moscú [Moscow], 1955. Negritas de JETA [JETA Bold].

"Even after the method has been discovered,." Engels underlines, on the other hand, "and according to him, the critique of Political Economy could be approached in two ways: the* **historical or the logical***. As in history, as in its literary reflection, things also develop, roughly, from the simplest to the most complex, the historical development of the literature on political economy provided a natural thread of critique for criticism , Then, in general terms, the economic categories would appear here in the same order as in their logical development [...]* **History often develops in jumps and zigzags***, and it should be followed in all its trajectory, which would not only collect many materials of little importance, but would often break the logical illation[...].* **Therefore, the only method indicated was the logical one. But this is in reality only the historical method, stripped only of its historical form and of disturbing contingencies. Where this history begins, the discursive process must begin as well, and the further development of the latter will be no more than the mirror image, in an abstract and theoretically consistent way, of the historical trajectory; A mirror image corrected, but corrected accord-**

(*) Se refiere a la dialéctica [It refers to the dialectic]. "La dialéctica no es otra cosa que la ciencia de las leyes generales del movimiento y del desarrollo en los campos de la naturaleza, de la sociedad humana y del pensamiento" ["Dialectics is nothing more than the science of the general laws of movement and development in the fields of nature, human society and thought."]. (F. Engels, *La subversión de la ciencia por el señor [The subversion of science by Mr.] Eugen Dühring ("Anti- Dühring")*, en **Obras fundamentales de** [In **Fundamental Works of] Carlos Marx y [and] Federico Engels**; Fondo de Cultura Económica [Fund of Economic Culture], Primera edición [First edition]; volumen [volume] 18; p. 123; México, 1986. "El hecho de que nuestro pensamiento subjetivo y el mundo objetivo se rigen por las mismas leyes, razón por la cual no pueden llegar, en última instancia, a resultados contradictorios entre sí, sino que estos resultados tienen que ser coincidentes, domina absolutamente todo nuestro pensar teórico. Constituye la premisa inconsciente e incondicional de éste" ["The fact that our subjective thinking and the objective world are governed by the same laws, which is why they cannot ultimately result in contradictory results, but that these results must be coincident, dominates absolutely all our Theoretical thinking. It constitutes the unconscious and unconditional premise of the latter"]. (Ibid., p. 486).

ing to the laws provided by the historical path itself; And thus, each factor can be studied at the point of development of its full maturity, in its classical form. With this method, we always start from the first and simplest relation that exists historically, in fact; therefore, here, of the first economic relationship with which we are .**. *Then we proceed to analyze it. Already in the mere fact of being a 'relationship', it is implied that it has two sides that 'relate to each other'.*

Each of these two sides is studied separately, from which they then reveal their reciprocal relationship and their interaction. We encounter contradictions, which call for a solution. But since we do not follow an abstract discursive process, which takes place exclusively in our heads, but a real sequence of events, actually and effectively occurring in some time or still happening, these contradictions will have arisen in practice and in it have probably also found their solution. And if we study the character of this solution we will see that it is achieved by creating a new relationship, whose two opposing sides we will have to develop now, and so on".[41]

** En el caso de la teoría del subdesarrollo, del "sistema centro-periferia", para decirlo con Prebisch, que surge de la nueva división internacional del trabajo que implanta la Revolución Industrial al producirse el proceso de integración de la economía mundial [In the case of the theory of underdevelopment, of the "center-periphery system", to put it with Prebisch, which arises from the new international division of labor that implanted the Industrial Revolution at the time of the process of integration of the world economy]. "El desarrollo y el subdesarrollo pueden comprenderse, entonces –subraya Sunkel-, como estructuras parciales, pero interdependientes, que conforman un sistema único" ["Development and underdevelopment can then be understood, as Sunkel points out, as partial but interdependent structures that form a single system."]. Osvaldo Sunkel, **El Subdesarrollo latinoamericano y la teoría del desarrollo** [Latin America Underdevelopment Theory], Siglo XXI Editores [21st Century Publishers], S.A., primera edición [first edition], p. 37; México, 1970.

(41) F. Engels, *La Contribución a la crítica de la Economía política [The Contribution to the Critique of Political Economy]*, de [of] Carlos Marx; **Obras escogidas [Selected Works]**; Editorial Progreso [Editorial Progress] , Tomo I [Volume I]; pp. 351-352; Moscú [Moscow], 1955. Negritas de JETA [JETA Bold].

"The Hegelian dialectic, that is to say, the most multilateral doctrine, richer in content and deeper in development," says Lenin, "was for Marx and Engels the greatest achievement of classical German philosophy. Evolution, they seemed unilateral and poor, deforming and mutilating the true developmental march in nature and in society[...]. It is a development that, apparently, repeats stages already traveled, but otherwise, on a higher basis ("Negation of negation"), a development, so to speak, in a spiral rather than a straight line, a development that operates in the form of leaps, through cataclysms and revolutions, which signify "interruptions of graduality"; Development that is the transformation of quantity into quality, internal impulses of development originated by contradiction, by the clash of the various forces and tendencies, acting on a given body, or within the limits of a given phenomenon or within a Society given; Interdependence, intimate and indissoluble concatenation of all aspects of each phenomenon (with the particularity that history constantly reveals new aspects), concatenation that offers a process of movement single, universal and subject to laws; Such are some features of dialectics, a theory much more permeated with content than the (usual) doctrine of evolution" [...] "Marx and I were almost the only ones who set ourselves the task of "saving" from the collapse of idealism, including Hegelianism the conscious dialectic to bring it to the materialist conception of nature. Nature is the confirmation of the dialectic, and we must thank the modern natural sciences for providing us with a collection of extraordinarily abundant data [and this was written before the discovery of radium, electrons, transformation of the elements, Etc.] and enriched each passing day, thereby demonstrating that nature moves, ultimately, through dialectical channels and not on the metaphysical lanes". [42]

---

(42) V.I. Lenin, Carlos Marx (Breve esbozo biográfico con una exposición del marxismo [Brief biographical sketch with an exposition of Marxism]) en **Obras**

"'For dialectical philosophy", writes Engels, *"there is nothing established once and for all, nothing absolute, consecrated, in everything it sees what is perishable, and leaves only the uninterrupted process of appearing and disappearing, of Infinite ascensional movement from the lower to the higher, and this very philosophy is a mere reflection of that process in the thinking brain.' Thus dialectics is, according to Marx, 'the science of the general laws of motion, External world as well as of human thought'. This revolutionary aspect of Hegelian philosophy is what Marx collects and develops [...] From the above philosophy stands the theory of thought and its laws, that is, formal logic and dialectic.' And dialectics, as Marx conceives it, and also according to Hegel, embraces what is now called the theory of knowledge or gnoseology"*[43]

What is involved, therefore, is to reproduce in the logic of thought the history of the phenomenon as it happened, so that each part occupies only the place and only the place that corresponds to it in the totality. Only in this way will we ascend from the simple to the complex, from the lower to the higher, from the abstract to the concrete, on the basis of the unity of the dialectic, the logic and the theory of knowledge.

Argentina is the classic home of underdevelopment. It is here that the phenomenon reaches the point of development of its full maturity. It is not possible, therefore, a theory of underdevelopment without taking from this country the main facts that serve as a basis for research .*, for to my point of view,

---

completas [In **Complete Works**], Editorial Cartago [Editorial Cartago], Tomo [Volume] XXI; p. 47,49,48; Buenos Aires, 1957.

(43) V.I. Lenin, Ob. Cit., p. 48.

* "Fundamentalmente –apunta Octavio Rodríguez-, los orígenes de la concepción del sistema centro-periferia se encuentran en trabajos de Raúl Prebisch previos a esa fecha (1949). Entre 1932 y 1943 dichos trabajos están relacionados con su participación en el manejo de la economía argentina y, por ende, con

which focuses on underdevelopment as a natural-historical process, what matters not Is a complete typology of under-developed countries of the region as Sunkel believed.**, but

---

esa experiencia específica. En los de la posguerra se percibe con claridad el intento de comparar la experiencia argentina con las de otras economías latino-americanas o subdesarrolladas, y de llegar así a generalizaciones sobre algunas tendencias y problemas que parecen serles comunes" ["Fundamentally," says Octavio Rodríguez, "the origins of the conception of the center-periphery system are found in works by Raúl Prebisch prior to that date (1949). Between 1932 and 1943 these works are related to his participation in the management of the Argentine economy and, therefore, with that specific experience. In the post-war period, the attempt to compare the Argentine experience with those of other Latin American or underdeveloped economies, and to reach generalizations about some tendencies and problems that seem to be common, is clearly perceived"]. (Octavio Rodríguez, **La teoría del subdesarrollo de la CEPAL [La teoría del subdesarrollo de la CEPAL]**; Siglo XXI [21st Century], 8° ed.; p. 19; México, D. F., 1993). "Mi ingreso en la Comisión Económica para América Latina de las Naciones Unidas, en 1949 –subraya Prebisch afirmando lo anterior-, ocurrió cuando mis ideas estaban llegando ya a la madurez, de modo que pude cristalizarlas en varios estudios publicados a principios de los años cincuenta, donde traté de presentar un diagnóstico de los problemas y de las sugestiones de políticas que servirían como opciones de las propuestas por la escuela ortodoxa. Gracias al horizonte más amplio que permitían mis nuevas responsabilidades, estos estudios no se aplicaban sólo a la Argentina sino al conjunto de la América Latina" ["My entry into the United Nations Economic Commission for Latin America in 1949," Prebisch points out, "occurred when my ideas were reaching maturity, so that I could crystallize them in several studies published in the early years Fifty, where I tried to present a diagnosis of the problems and the policy suggestions that would serve as options of the proposals by the Orthodox school. Thanks to the broader horizon allowed by my new responsibilities, these studies applied not only to Argentina but to Latin America as a whole"]. (Raúl Prebisch, *Cinco etapas de mi pensamiento sobre el desarrollo [Five stages of my thinking about development] (ensayo presentado en un seminario del Banco Mundial [Essays presented at a World Bank seminar])*, en CEPAL [in ECLAC], **Raúl Prebisch: un aporte al estudio de su pensamiento [A contribution to the study of his thinking]**, LC/G.1461, p. 14; Santiago de Chile, marzo de [March] 1987. Publicación de las Naciones Unidas [United Nations publication], N° de venta [Sales No.] S.87.II.G.6.

** El período del modelo de crecimiento hacia afuera –indica Sunkel refiriéndose a algunas de las principales insuficiencias de su libro *El subdesarrollo latinoamericano y la teoría del desarrollo-* fue estudiado país por país y no sólo en sus aspectos económicos, sino también -aunque con menos profundidad- en los sociales y políticos. Un análisis similar para el período posterior implicaba

the **tendencies**, the **very laws** that act and impose themselves as an unavoidable necessity. The most developed underdeveloped country, in this case Argentina, which had already gone through all the phases of its historical formation after World War II, was only showing at least an underdeveloped mirror of its own future.

---

examinar las diferencias específicas de los procesos de industrialización o de sustitución de importaciones en cada uno de los países del área, lo que hubiera permitido continuar con la tipología [The period of the outward growth model, Sunkel says, referring to some of the major shortcomings of his book, *Latin American Underdevelopment and Development Theory*, was studied country by country and not only in its economic aspects but also - albeit with less depth - in the social and political. A similar analysis for the later period implied examining the specific differences in the processes of industrialization or import substitution in each of the countries of the area, which would have allowed continuing the typology]. (Osvaldo Sunkel, Ob. Cit., p. 10).

III. THE SLOW SPREAD OF TECHNICAL PROGRESS IN THE PERIPHERY AS A POINT OF DEPARTURE AND MAIN WEAKNESS OF THE CONCEPTION OF UNDERDEVELOPMENT OF ECLAC

1. THE CENTRAL AXIS OF THE THEORY UNDERDEVELOPMENT OF PREBISCH-ECLAC

The slow spread of technical progress in the periphery, perpetuated by the new international division of labor that implanted the Industrial Revolution (between producing countries and producing countries of primary products and market of those), when the process of integration of the economy took place Is the main weakness of ECLAC's theory of underdevelopment. This point of view of ECLAC, the cornerstone of all its theory, becomes, in turn, its starting point and starting point, at the same time, of its intense and acute ideological struggle with the United States, hegemonic center principal of the **"center-periphery system"**. At the root of this ideological antagonism lies the decision to promote industrialization, against the economic interests of the main hegemonic center, as the only valid way for the underdeveloped countries, specifically in the region, to take advantage of the advantages of technical progress. **Industrialization** would make it possible to achieve a more dynamic and autonomous development, and less vulnerable to the outside world, as well as absorb labor, increase productivity and gradually improve the standard of living of the population.

The intense and acute ideological struggle that took place throughout the 1950s placed ECLAC and the State Department in the antipode of contradiction, to the point of endangering the very existence of the institution.

Let us see, then, the crux of the matter.

"The universal PROPAGATION of technical progress from the original countries to the rest of the world has been relatively slow and irregular, if we take as a point of view the one of each generation. In the long period from the Industrial Revolution to the First World War, new forms of production in which technology has been ceaselessly manifested have covered only a small proportion of the world's population. The movement begins in Great Britain, continues with varying degrees of intensity in the European continent, acquires an extraordinary impulse in the United States and finally includes Japan, when this country is quick to assimilate the western ways of producing. Thus formed the great industrial centers of the world, around which the periphery of the new system, vast and heterogeneous, took little part in the improvement of productivity. Within this periphery, technical progress only engages in small sectors of its enormous population, since it generally does not penetrate but where it is necessary to produce food and raw materials at low cost, destined to those large industrial centers".[1]

---

(1) Raúl Prebisch, *Crecimiento, desequilibrio y disparidades [Growth, imbalance and disparities]: interpretación del proceso de desarrollo económico [interpretation of the process of economic development]* (Primera parte del *Estudio Económico de la América Latina, 1949*, CEPAL [First part of the *Economic Survey of Latin America, 1949*, ECLAC]); tomado de la **Lectura** [Taken from **Reading**] **N° 46*, La obra de Prebisch en la CEPAL [Prebisch's work in**

In this view, almost all authors of ECLAC agree.

"The world view of the international economy", says Celso Furtado, expressing this consensus, "which affirmed the existence of a structural rupture caused by the slow propagation of technical progress and which was perpetuated by the international division of labor, **was the main theoretical contribution of Prebisch and constituted the starting point of the theory of underdevelopment, which assumed a preponderant position in post-war Latin America thinking. For Prebisch, underdevelopment stems from 'the concentration of technical progress and its fruits in export-oriented economic activities', giving rise to heterogeneous social structures 'by virtue of which a large part of the population is kept apart from development'".**[2]

"Trying to find an explanation of these phenomena", Prebisch adds elsewhere, "in those years I emphasized the fact that the countries of Latin America are part of a system of international economic relationships that I call the center-periphery system. Actually, this concept had been spinning in my mind for some time. At the beginning I assigned it a cyclical character, considering that it reflected the active role of industrial centers and the passivity of the periphery, where the economic fluctuations of the centers intensified their consequences. There was indeed an economic constellation centered on the industrialized countries favored by this position,

---

ECLAC, Selección de Adolfo Gurrieri en dos partes [Selection of Adolfo Gurrieri in two parts], de la serie Lecturas de El Trimestre Económico [from the series of Economic Quarter Readings]; Fondo de Cultura Económica, primera edición [first edition]; Primera parte [First pat] (El programa inicial en la CEPAL [The initial program in ECLAC]), p. 156; México, 1982.

(2) Celso Furtado, *La cosmovisión de Prebisch [Prebisch's worldview]*, en Banco Interamericano de Desarrollo [at the Inter-American Development Bank], **El legado de [The legacy of] Raúl Prebisch**; Enrique V. Iglesias Editor [Publisher]; pp. 52-53; Washington, D.C., 1993.Negritas de JETA [JETA Bold].

supported by its previous advance in technical progress, who organized the system as a whole to serve its own interests. The producing and exporting countries of raw materials were thus connected with the center, according to their natural resources, so that they formed a vast and heterogeneous periphery, incorporated in the system in different form and breadth. While my diagnosis of the situation in Latin American countries, he added finally, was based on my critique of the pattern of development oriented outward, which in my opinion did not allow the full development of such countries, the development policy I proposed was geared towards establishment of a new pattern of development that would overcome the limitations of the previous pattern; this new form of development would have as main objective the industrialization. In fact, the economic policy that I proposed tried to give a theoretical justification for the industrialization policy that was already being followed (especially in the large countries of Latin America), to encourage other countries to follow it as well, Provide them with an orderly strategy for their execution". [3]

*"In other words," remarks Octavio Rodríguez, "centers and peripheries are historically constituted as a result of the way technical progress propagates in the world economy. In the centers, the indirect methods of production that the technical progress generates diffuse in a relatively short time to the whole productive apparatus. At the periphery, an initial backwardness begins, and as the so-called **outward development** period elapses, new techniques are only implanted in the*

---

(3) Raúl Prebich, *Cinco etapas de mi pensamiento sobre el desarrollo [Five stages of my thinking about development] (ensayo presentado en un seminario del Banco Mundial [essay presented at a World Bank seminar])*; en CEPAL [in ECLAC], **Raúl Prebisch: un aporte al estudio de su pensamiento [a contribution to the study of his thinking]**, LC/G.1461, Santiago de Chile, marzo de [March] 1987; pp. 14-15. Publicación de las Naciones Unidas [United Nations publication], N° de venta [Sales No] S.87.II.G.6. Negritas de Prebisch [Bold of Prebisch].

exporting sectors of primary products and in some economic activities directly related to exports, which coexist with lagging sectors in terms of the penetration of new techniques and the level of labor productivity". [4]

---

(4) Octavio Rodríguez, **La teoría del subdesarrollo de la CEPAL [The Theory of Underdevelopment of ECLAC]**; Siglo XXI [21st Century], 8° ed.; p. 25; México, D. F., 1993. Negritas de [Bold by] Octavio Rodríguez. No hay que olvidar que de acuerdo con el razonamiento de las ventajas económicas de la división internacional del trabajo el fruto del progreso técnico tiende a repartirse equitativamente, ya sea por la disminución de los precios o por el alza equivalente de los ingresos. Los países de producción primaria obtienen, por tanto, su parte en aquel fruto y no necesitan industrializarse. Antes bien, su menor eficiencia les haría perder las ventajas clásicas del intercambio. Más aun, el progreso técnico parece haber sido mayor en la industria que en la producción primaria de los países de la periferia. En consecuencia, si los precios hubieran descendido en armonía con la mayor productividad, la baja habría tenido que ser menor en los productos primarios que en los industriales, de manera que la relación de precios ente ambos hubiera ido mejorando persistentemente en favor de los países de la periferia conforme se desarrollaba la disparidad de productividades. Empero, esto no es lo que ha ocurrido en la realidad. Desde los años setenta del siglo hasta antes de la segunda Guerra Mundial, la relación de precios se ha movido constantemente en contra de la producción primaria. Un razonamiento simple sobre este fenómeno nos permite formular, indica Prebisch, las siguientes consideraciones [It should not be forgotten that according to the reasoning of the economic advantages of the international division of labor, the fruit of technical progress tends to be equitably distributed, either by the fall in prices or by the equivalent increase in income. The countries of primary production therefore obtain their share in that fruit and do not need to industrialize. Rather, their lower efficiency would make them lose the classic advantages of exchange. Moreover, technical progress seems to have been greater in industry than in primary production in peripheral countries. Consequently, if prices had fallen in line with higher productivity, the fall would have had to be lower in primary than in industrial products, so that the price relationship between them would have been steadily improving in favor of developing countries. The periphery as the disparity of productivities developed. However, this is not what has happened in reality. From the seventies of the century until before the Second World War, the price relationship has been constantly moving against primary production. A simple reasoning on this phenomenon allows us to formulate, Prebisch says, the following considerations]: *"Primero: los precios no han bajado conforme al progreso técnico, pues mientras por un lado el costo tendía a bajar, a causa del aumento de la productividad, subían por otra parte los ingresos de los empresarios y de los factores productivos. Cuando el ascenso de los ingresos fue más intenso que el de la productividad los precios subieron en vez de bajar. Segundo: si el crecimiento de los ingresos, en los centros industriales y en la periferia, hubiese sido proporcional al aumen-*

Convinced of the certainty of his thesis, in the early 1960s,

---

to de las respectivas productividades, la relación de precios entre los productos primarios y los productos finales de la industria no hubiese sido diferente de la que habría existido si los precios hubiesen bajado estrictamente de acuerdo con la productividad. Y dada la mayor productividad de la industria, la relación de precios se habría movido en favor de los productos primarios. Tercero: como en realidad la relación, según se ha visto, se ha movido en contra de los productos primarios, entre los años setenta del siglo pasado y los años treinta del presente, es obvio que los ingresos de los empresarios y factores productivos han crecido en los centros más que el aumento de la productividad, y en la periferia menos que el respectivo aumento de la misma. **En otros términos, mientras los centros han retenido íntegramente el fruto del progreso técnico de su industria, los países de la periferia les han traspasado una parte del fruto de su propio progreso técnico** *["First, prices have not fallen according to technical progress, because while on the one hand the cost tended to fall, because of the increase in productivity, on the other hand, the incomes of the entrepreneurs and the factors of production went up. When the rise in income was more intense than that of productivity, prices went up instead of going down. Second, if the income growth in industrial centers and in the periphery had been proportional to the increase in the respective productivities, the price relationship between the primary products and the final products of industry would not have been different from that of would have existed if prices had fallen strictly according to productivity. And given the increased productivity of the industry, the price relationship would have moved in favor of primary products. Thirdly, since the relationship has, as we have seen, moved against primary products, between the 1970s and the 1930s, it is obvious that the incomes of entrepreneurs and productive factors have grown In the centers rather than the increase of productivity, and in the periphery less than the respective increase of the same.* **In other words, while the centers have completely retained the fruit of the technical progress of their industry, the countries of the periphery have transferred to them a part of the fruit of their own technical progress]"**. {Raúl Prebisch, *El desarrollo económico de la América Latina y algunos de sus principales problemas [The economic development of Latin America and some of its main problems]* (escrito en 1949 como introducción al Estudio económico de la América Latina 1948. Posteriormente fue publicado en el Boletín económico de la América Latina, vol. VII, núm. 1, febrero de 1962 [written in 1949 as an introduction to the Economic Survey of Latin America, 1948. It was later published in the Economic Bulletin of Latin America, Vol. VII, no. 1, February 1962]); tomado de la **Lectura** [Taken from **Reading**] 46*, **La obra de Prebisch en la CEPAL [Prebisch's work in ECLAC]**, selección de Adolfo Gurrieri en dos partes [Adolfo Gurrieri's selection in two parts]; de la Serie de Lecturas de El Trimestre Económico [Of the Economic Quarter Readings Series]; Fondo de Cultura Económica, primera edición [first edition]; Primera parte [First part] (El programa inicial en la CEPAL [The initial program in ECLAC]); p. 109; México, 1982}. Negritas de Prebisch [Bold of Prebisch].

in the years 1960-1961, in the midst of industrialization in the most advanced countries of the region, Prebisch reaffirmed:

*"Historically technical progress has not spread evenly, thus contributing to the division of the world economy into industrial centers on the one hand, and peripheral countries of primary production on the other, with consequent differences in the growth of entry. We are now in a **period of transition** in which that division is gradually being erased, but it will be long before it disappears altogether. **As technical progress, originally limited to the primary export sectors and related activities, is increasingly extended on the periphery and encompasses other sectors, the need for industrialization is felt [...] Unless supported by a Vigorous process of industrialization and increasing productivity in industry** - adds the author - **the technical advance in primary production as an alternative to** industrialization - in order to improve living standards - will be counterproductive, since the fruits of Such progress will generally be transferred from peripheral countries to the outside world. The greater the inelasticity of the demand for peripheral exports, the greater the proportion of profits to be transferred"* [5]

---

(5) Raúl Prebisch, *La política comercial en los países insuficientemente desarrollados [Trade policy in underdeveloped countries].* Desde el punto de vista latinoamericano *[From the Latin America point of view]*; tomado de la **Lectura 46*** [Taken from **Reading 46***], **La obra de Prebisch en la CEPAL [Prebisch's work at ECLAC]**, selección de Adolfo Gurrieri en dos partes [Selection of Adolfo Gurrieri in two parts]; de la Serie de Lecturas de El Trimestre Económico [Of the Economic Quarter Reading Series]; Fondo de Cultura Económica [Fund of Economic Culture], primera edición [first edition]; Segunda parte [second part] (Esfuerzo interno y cooperación internacional [Internal effort and international cooperation]: el programa de desarrollo en los años setenta [The development program in the 1970's])); pp. 442, 443; México, 1982. Negritas de Prebisch [Bold of Prebisch]. Gurrieri señala que el Artículo fue publicado en la *Revista Economía*, de la Universidad de Chile [Gurrieri points out that the article was published in the *Economics Journal* of the University of Chile], vols. [volume]. XIX y XX [19 & 20], años [years] 1960-1961, núms. [numbers]. 69 y 70. La versión en inglés apareció en la [The English version appeared in

This conception of underdevelopment as **a structural rupture caused by the slow propagation of technical progress and perpetuated by the international division of labor, the main theoretical contribution of Prebisch and the point of departure of the theory of underdevelopment, as Furtado points out, seems to me to be completely inaccurate.**

Contrary to what Prebisch maintains, the technical progress expressed in the Industrial Revolution, that is, in the discovery of **machinery**, the greatest technological leap that humanity had known until then, **and not the disparity as this leap propagates technological**, is the cause of the emergence of underdevelopment. From the moment the extraction of coal and iron, the processing of metals and transportation, and the creation of all the general conditions of production corresponding to the great industry, this system of capitalist production takes on an elasticity, a capacity Sudden and intensive expansion that only stops before the obstacles that oppose the raw materials and the market. The machinery determines, on the

---

the] *American Economic Review*, núm. [number]. 3, 1959. Prebisch agradece la crítica valiosa y sus constructivas sugerencias a los señores [Prebisch appreciates the valuable criticism and his constructive suggestions to the gentlemen] Hollisb Chenery, profesor de la Universidad de Stanford [Professor at Stanford University], y [and] Louis N. Swenson, subdirector de la Comisión Económica para América Latina [Deputy director of the Economic Commission for Latin America], así como a los señores [As well as the gentlemen] Hans Singer y [and] Sidney Dell, del Departamento Económico y Social de las Naciones Unidas [Of the Economic and Social Department of the United Nations]. Me es grato dejar constancia aquí –agrega Prebisch- de la coincidencia de ideas de este trabajo con las líneas generales de la monografía del doctor Singer [I am pleased to record here, "adds Prebisch," the coincidence of ideas in this work with the general lines of the monograph of Dr. Singer], *La industrialización [The industrialization]: la otra cara de la moneda [The other side of the coin]*, preparada para la reciente reunión del Grupo de Trabajo de ECAFE [Prepared for the recent meeting of the ECAFE Working Group], sobre "El papel de la industrialización en el desarrollo económico" [On "The role of industrialization in economic development"], monografía que recibí después de terminado el presente artículo [Monograph that I received after the completion of this article].

one hand, a direct increase of the raw materials, at the same time that the cheapening of the articles produced to machines and the transformation operated in means of communication and of transport create all the technical and material premises for the conquest of foreign markets. And it is in these historical conditions that the very nature of the capitalist system is maturing, that the process of integration of the world economy is being carried out. On the basis of this integration, Marx stresses, ***"a new international division of labor is being implemented, adjusted to the major centers of large industry, division of labor that makes a part of the planet a preferred field of agricultural production for the needs of another part organized as an industrial production field"*** [6]

The division of the world economy into industrial centers on the one hand, and peripheral countries of primary production on the other, is not the product of the uneven propagation of technical progress, as Prebisch argues, **but the inexorable result of the new international division Of the work implanted by the Industrial Revolution to trigger the process of integration of the world economy.** In other words, the **"center-periphery system"** is not the result of a structural rupture caused by the slow spread of technical progress and perpetuated by the international division of labor, but the opposite, **the new international division of labor is the basis Explains the slow spread of technical progress in the periphery. Of course, this new international division of labor which implements the Industrial Revolution is a historical-natural, inexorable law of the capitalist system. Men cannot abolish, destroy or transform the laws of nature, nor the laws of the development of society. Its function is to discover them, to know them and to take advantage of them in the interest of society. To deny the laws of social**

---

(6) Caros Marx, **El Capital [The Capital]**; Editorial Nacional de Cuba [National Editorial of Cuba]; Tomo [Volume] I; p. 403; La Habana [Havana], 1962.

phenomena is to renounce the possibility of influencing the march of these phenomena and governing the course of events.

Prebisch, however, under the influence of the mirage of the process of import substitution that emerged in the region during World War I, the Great Depression of 1929-30 and World War II, chose to challenge that historical-natural law, objective and Inexorable of the capitalist system.

*"**If this economic constellation to which the world had come before the first war**," Prebisch points out, "**it could be considered as the ideal system of the division of labor, it is clear that everything that departs from its canons would have to be considered as a deviation from the normal mode of running the economy.** However, there could be no reason of scientific validity to consider that constellation was definitive. Only at that time had a stage of singular importance been achieved in the process of growth of the world economy, which, no matter how great its effects, could scarcely be termed the final phase, since it was in some way outside it The vast field of the periphery, with enormous possibilities of assimilating technical progress to raise the very precarious standard of living of its large masses of population".*[7]

As we can see, Prebisch was convinced that the vigorous process of industrialization undertaken by the more advanced countries of the periphery would gradually erase that division of the world economy into industrial centers on the one hand and peripheral countries of primary production on the other.

---

(7) Raúl Prebisch, *Crecimiento, desequilibrio y disparidades [Growth, imbalances and disparities]: interpretación del proceso de desarrollo económico [Interpretation of the economic development process]* (Primera parte del *Estudio Económico de la América Latina, 1949*, CEPAL [First part of the *Economic Survey of Latin America, 1949*, ECLAC]); en [in] Ob. Cit. p. 156. Negritas de Prebisch [Bold of Prebisch].

However, the process of import substitution was unsuccessful and what appeared to be a prolonged **transition period**, disappeared and, in the late 1960s and early 1970s, gave way to so-called the dependence that, within the ECLAC, replaced the Prebisch-ECLAC theory of underdevelopment.

"**Consequently**," says Osvaldo Sunkel, reaffirming the failure of the import substitution process, "**the development strategy through import substitution industrialization** *that should have freed the economy from its strong dependence on primary and capital export and technology has not only failed to achieve these goals, it has in fact aggravated the situation and dependent nature of our economies".[8]*

*"From the failure of these policies," added José Villamil, "and as a continuation of a long tradition of critical thinking in Latin America, a new approach to development problems emerged, which was called the dependency approach. **This new approach sought to integrate class analysis with ECLAC visions and, in addition, to broaden the vision of the problem away from the strictly economist approach that had prevailed".[9]***

---

(8) Osvaldo Sunkel, *La naturaleza de la dependencia latinoamericana [The Nature f Latin American Dependency]*, en Serie de Lecturas de El Trimestre económico [in Economic Quarter Series], **Lectura N° [Lecture No] 30****, **Economía internacional [International Economics]**, René Villarreal (compilador [compiler]); Fondo de Cultura Económica [Fund of Economic Culture], primera edición [first edition]; p. 275-276; México, 1979. Negritas de JETA [JETA Bold],

(9) José J. Villamil, *Introducción [Introduction]*, en Serie de Lecturas de El Trimestre económico [Series of Readings of The Economic Quarter], **Lectura N° [Lecture No] 37, Capitalismo transnacional y desarrollo nacional [Transnational Capitalism and National Development]**, José J. Villamil (compilador [compiler]); Fondo de Cultura Económica [Fund of Economic Culture], primera edición en español [first edition in Spanish], corregida y aumentada [corrected and enlarged]; p. 11; México, 1981. Negritas de JETA [JETA Bold].

Hence, Prebisch's claim that the beginning of the process of import substitution is not a "**transition period** in which the division is gradually being erased, but it will be a long time before it disappears altogether". Nor is it true that "technical progress, originally limited to primary export sectors and related activities, will increasingly extend to the periphery of industrial sectors".

It is evident, on the other hand, neither the so-called **theory of "dependence"** of ECLAC by Fernando Henrique Cardoso and Enzo Faletto, nor the attempts of the mature work of Raúl Prebisch, **Peripheral capitalism. Crisis and transformation**, integrate, despite their good intentions, the **analysis of class** with the visions of ECLAC.

*"Rightly so," says Prebisch in the Prologue to the Theory of Underdevelopment of ECLAC, "Octavio Rodríguez highlights in his book the limitations of ECLAC's theories, which are strictly economic theories, with some circumstantial incursion into other fields. , Sociologists and economists have been mismatched for a long time, thinking with some suspicion who dared to enter the enclosure that corresponded to the other. Well, I have made a modest essay in which I am still working. , To interpret peripheral development as a complex phenomenon of a dynamic nature that encompasses technical, economic, social, political and cultural elements. This all goes beyond the scope of economic theory, with which I expose myself to the indifference of economists and nonconformity. However it may be, he adds later, this is new theoretical venture of mine, begun by leaving aside executive responsibilities, represents another phase in the development of ECLAC thought and, as such, cannot escape our original concept that has been called the **center-periphery scheme"**. [10]*

---

(10) Raúl Prebisch, *Prologo* a la obra de [*Prologue* to the work of] Octavio Rodríguez, **La teoría del subdesarrollo de la CEPAL [The Theory of Under-**

Unfortunately, the renewal of his thinking, or put another way, in his neo-structuralist version, his work matures **Peripheral Capitalism. Crisis and transformation** does not represent, from the point of view of the specific social classes of peripheral capitalism, any substantive advance.

Prebisch attempts to make the leap to **class analysis** but fails and continues to be caught by his theory of the slow spread of technical progress in the periphery, that is, in the conception of political economy as relations between things (between technical progress and The distribution of increases in productivity) or between things and man and not between people and, ultimately, between classes. As we pointed out in the previous work, *"Economics does not deal with things, but with relationships between people and, ultimately, between classes; although these relationships are always linked to things and appear as things".*[11]

The contradictions of Raúl Prebisch in his attempts to overcome his limitations in the analysis of classes are remarkable. Here are some examples.

"If the technical progress of industrial centers and their gradual spread to the rest of the world bring new problems at the international level," *says the author, "[...] they also bring them in developing countries [...] Three are in general - he adds, later on, the great obstacles that stand in the way of the spread of technical progress and, therefore, the increase in productivity and per capita income in developing countries:*

---

development of ECLAC], Siglo xxi editores [21st Century Publishers], octava edición [8th edition], p. x-xi; México, 1993.) Negritas de Prebisch [Bold of Prebisch].

(11) F. Engels, *La Contribución a la crítica de la Economía política [The Contribution to the Critique of Political Economy], de [of] Carlos Marx;* **Obras escogidas [Selected Works];** Editorial Progreso [Progress], Tomo [Volume]I; p. 352; Moscú [Moscow], 1955.

land tenure; the lack of social mobility and ignorance of the masses, and the concentration of income in relatively small groups of the population [...] The weakness of the development drive in many peripheral countries, *he finally indicates*, **is a consequence of all those internal factors that Are integrated into a particular social structure, in addition to external factors that strangle growth. Development requires changes in the forms of production and in the structure of the economy that could not be operated without the transformation of that social structure giving way to the forces of technical progress".**[12]

"The appropriation of the fruit of technical progress in peripheral capitalism," he affirms elsewhere, "is largely the arbitrary result of a game of power relations that arises from the social structure [...] I maintain here that the origin of all this, if it allows me to simplify it, it is that this fruit of the greater productivity that brings the propagation of the technique of the centers in the periphery tends to concentrate to a large extent in the upper strata of income, mainly by virtue of the economic power of these stratum".[13]

---

(12) Raúl Prebisch, *Nueva política comercial para el desarrollo [New trade policy for development]* (Informe presentado por R. Prebisch a la Segunda Conferencia de las Naciones Unidas sobre Comercio y Desarrollo, Ginebra, 1964, en su carácter de Secretario General de la misma [Report submitted by R. Prebisch to the Second United Nations Conference on Trade and Development, Geneva, 1964, in his capacity as Secretary-General of the Conference]); tomado de la **Lectura** [Taken from **reading**] **46** (La obra de Prebisch en la CEPAL [Prebisch's work at ECLAC]**, selección de Adolfo Gurrieri en dos partes [Selection of Adolfo Gurrieri in two parts]), de la Serie de Lecturas de El Trimestre Económico [Of the Economic Quarter Reading Series]; Fondo de Cultura Económica [Fund of Economic Culture], primera edición [first edition]; Segunda parte [Second part] (Esfuerzo interno y cooperación internacional el programa de desarrollo en los años setenta [Internal effort and international cooperation the development program in the 1970s])); pp. 345-346; México, 1982. Negritas de Prebisch [Prebisch Bold].

(13) Raúl Prebisch, *Estructura socioeconómica y crisis del sistema (reflexiones al cumplirse nuestros primeros treinta años [Socioeconomic structure and crisis*

"We have characterized, finally, in his mature work, the peripheral development as a process of irradiation and propagation from the centers of techniques, consumption patterns and other cultural forms, ideas, ideologies and institutions. All this in a fundamentally different social structure. Therein lays the root of the contradictions from which the great internal failures of peripheral capitalism arise". [14]

Regardless of the fate of the import substitution process, industrialization became the central focus of ECLAC's development strategy in the early 1950s.

"Unless supported by a vigorous process of industrialization and increasing productivity in industry," *Prebisch points out,* **"technical advance in primary production as an alternative to industrialization, in order to improve living standards, will be counterproductive,** *since the fruits of such progress will generally be transferred from peripheral countries to the outside world".* [15]

---

of the system (reflections on our first thirty years))]); en **Revista de la CEPAL** [in **ECLAC Magazine**]; pp. 168-169; Segundo semestre de [Second Semester in] 1978).

(14) Raúl Prebisch, **Capitalismo periférico [Peripheral capitalism]. Crisis y transformación [Crisis and transformation]**, Fondo de Cultura Económica [Fund of Economic Culture], primera edición [first edition]; p. 211; México, D. F., 1981.

(15) Raúl Prebisch, La política comercial en los países insuficientemente desarrollados. Desde el punto de vista latinoamericano [Trade policy in underdeveloped countries. From the Latin American point of view] (Artículo publicado en la Revista Economía [Article published in Economy Magazine], de la Universidad de Chile [of the University of Chile], vols [Volume]. XIX y XX, años [years] 1960-1961, núms [numbers] 69 y 70); tomado de la **Lectura** [taken from **Reading**] **46*, La obra de Prebisch en la CEPAL [Prebisch's work at ECLAC]**, selección de Adolfo Gurrieri en dos partes [Selection of Adolfo Gurrieri in two parts]), de la Serie de Lecturas de El Trimestre Económico [Of the Economic Quarter Reading Series]; Fondo de Cultura Económica [Fund of Economic Culture], primera edición [first edition]; Primera parte [first part] (El programa

This point of view of ECLAC, the cornerstone of his theory, becomes, in turn, the starting point of an intense and acute ideological struggle with the main hegemonic center. At the root of this ideological antagonism lies the decision to promote industrialization against the economic interests of the main hegemonic center as the only valid way for underdeveloped countries to take advantage of the benefits of technical progress. **Industrialization** would make it possible to achieve a more dynamic and autonomous development, and less vulnerable to the outside world, as well as to absorb labor force, increase productivity and gradually improve the standard of living of the population.

2. THE GREAT DEPRESSION OF 1929-30 AND THE PREBISCH RUPTURE WITH THE NEO-CLASSIC SCHOOL.

In point I.1. *"The neoclassical frustration"* of the **fifth part** of his mature work, Prebisch states:

*"In this paper I have tried to explore new ways of interpreting peripheral capitalism. Why do it? Why not examine this phenomenon in the light of neoclassical teachings? And instead of thinking about fundamental transformations, will not the solution be to firmly adhere to such teachings, to let market forces act without artificial interventions, in order to achieve the most efficient allocation of productive resources and the rational distribution of the product thus achieved? **As I have repeatedly stated, I was a neoclassical of deep convictions I believe, and still believe, in the advantages of an ideal competition and in the technical efficiency of the market,***

---

inicial en la CEPAL [The initial program in ECLAC]), p. 443; México, 1982. Negritas de Prebisch [Prebisch Bold].

and also in its great political significance. But peripheral capitalism is very different from all that. And the observation of reality has persuaded me that these theories do not allow us to interpret or attack the great problems that derive from their functioning. *I have made a great effort to escape these theories and to explain with intellectual independence the phenomena of peripheral development; And in trying to do it I have found great resistances, and I keep finding them. The neoclassicists tried to systematize and give logical consistency to the core ideas of their classical precursors. They thus formulated their great doctrinal conception of economic equilibrium and the interdependence of all the elements involved in the game of economics. As I once remembered, during my youth these theories seduced me by their precision and mathematical elegance; and also by its persuasive force. They demonstrated that the free play of the forces of the economy, without any interference, led to the best use of productive factors for the benefit of the whole community, both in the international arena and in the internal development. And there was in them an underlying ethical element which undoubtedly contributed to their intellectual prestige. But in their search for rigor, in the disdain that their adepts manifested by those who in those days called literary economists, they managed to discard from their reasoning important elements of social and political reality, cultural reality and historical development of collectivities. And by displaying a persistent effort of doctrinal asepsis, they developed their reasoning in the void, outside time and space.* **If, when elaborated, they seemed to represent a significant scientific advance, considered in the light of capitalist evolution, they involve a true scientific aberration, especially when they try to interpret the phenomena of the periphery.** *These theories, however, contain positive elements that should in no way be disdained. I am not surprised by the neoclassical enlightenment of a plethora of Latin American economists who, indoctrinated in certain* *schools of the centers, are now trying to apply their teachings to the practice of peripheral development. And I also understand their repudiation of interventions that, far from correcting those flaws in the system, often make them more disturbing and often lead to their bureaucratic perversion.* **If neoclassical economists were limited to elevating their constructions in the ethereal world, but without pretending that this is the reality, this would constitute a respectable intellectual amusement, admirable at times for the virtuosity of some of its eminent exhibitors beyond the seas. But the situation is very different when in these peripheral lands the aim is to explain development, regardless of the social structure, the historical retardation of the peripheral development, the surplus and all the characteristics of peripheral capitalism that I have occupied previously. For it is clear and convincing that the spontaneous play of economics cannot lead to equilibrium.** *The capacity for intellectual survival of neoclassical theories is explained, especially when it's logical rigor is demonstrated by the system of equations introduced by Walras and Pareto, the starting point of the later evolution of such theories. It is worth remembering at the moment when these vigorous shoots appear in some Latin American countries. I really deplore that we could not use those doctrines. It would be wonderful to let the forces of the economy spontaneously lead to the efficiency and equity of the system, regardless of the deliberate and very complex commitment to act upon them.* **Moreover, I confess that I would be willing to temporarily justify certain collective sacrifices if we thereby definitively cleared the obstacles to development. But it is not so, and I feel the intellectual need - and the moral responsibility - to present the reasons that have led me to abandon orthodoxy. But I am always ready for dialogue and look forward to it. And I would not hesitate to acknowledge my departure, to capitulate and to amend myself, if from the dialogue there were valid reasons for doing so. The reasons**

why I have long disagreed, with neoclassical theories concern the distribution of income, the accumulation of capital, and the role of the market in relationship to internal development and international exchange [...] ..I suppose, And I think that these theories are also far from explaining the phenomena of the capitalist development of the centers, I will confine myself exclusively to the periphery, first of all because I think I know it better, and perhaps because I do not have to fight on two fronts simultaneously, of which, of course, it would not be exempt".[16]

It is important to emphasize, however, that the break with the neoclassical school occurs some years before its incorporation to ECLAC in 1949.

"In the elaboration of my ideas"[...] Prebisch says, "The great depression of the world was greatly influenced. I was forced, then, by the necessity of facing the very adverse repercussions of this phenomenon, I had to throw away neoclassical theories of which I had nurtured in my university youth. The teachings of that crisis made me reflect later on peripheral development, its great external vulnerability and relationship with the centers".[17]

"During those hectic years of the depression," he added elsewhere, "I exercised some influence over the economic policy of my country, Argentina, first as Undersecretary of Finance and then as central banker. ***In the 1930s I recommended orthodox anti-inflationary measures to eliminate the fiscal deficit and suppress inflationary trends, but at the***

---

(16) Raúl Prebisch, **Capitalismo periférico [Peripheral capitalism]. Crisis y transformación [Crisis and transformation]**; Fondo de Cultura Económica [Fund of Economic Culture], primera edición [first edition]; pp. 247-249; México, D. F., 1981. Las negritas son de JETA [The bold ones are from JETA].

(17) Ibid., p. 25.

same time I moved away from orthodoxy when I faced serious balance of payments disequilibrium and advised a resolute policy of industrialization and other targeted measures to that end".[18]

In 1931 assumes like undersecretary of Property and is forced to apply policies to face the crisis. During that year and the following the government policy combines orthodox measures, such as reduction of public spending, tax increase and credit reduction, with others of a heterodox nature such as authorizing rediscount operations to improve the situation of banks raise their tariffs to offset the imbalance of the balance of payments and reduce the fiscal deficit, control the exchange to defend the value of the peso in relation to gold and introduce the income tax to improve tax collection.

"These unorthodox measures which Prebisch helped to formulate and implement in 1931 were always presented as transitory and extraordinary, so that they were accepted by the rest of the members of the government and by the economic elite, where the orthodox tendency in economic policy prevailed. They were always presented as the imposition of a reality that had been transformed; when it returned to normal they would be abandoned and returned to good doctrine. To them must be added a project for the creation of a Central Bank which Prebisch wrote in 1931 - and the Executive did not dare to present to Congress fearing that he would consider it too interventionist and permanent - where he proposed to regulate not only the inflationary tendencies in the cycles

---

(18) Raúl Prebisch, *Cinco etapas de mi pensamiento sobre el desarrollo [Five stages of my thinking about development]* (ensayo presentado en un seminario del Banco Mundial [Essay presented at a World Bank seminar]), en CEPAL [in ECLAC], **Raúl Prebisch: un aporte al estudio de su pensamiento [A contribution to the study of his thinking]**, LC/G.1461, p. 13; Santiago de Chile, marzo de [March] 1987. Publicación de las Naciones Unidas [United Nations publication], N° de venta [Sales No] S.87.II.G.6. Negritas de JETA [JETA Bold].

but also -heterodoxy unacceptable- recessive in the waning. Therefore, he very quickly abandons the gold standard and turns to heterodoxy, when he still believed that the crisis was only a cyclical decline; it no longer accepts that the 'liquidation' of assets is an acceptable resource to overcome the crisis and that full freedom of action must be given to the automatic mechanisms of the market. The rapidity of this change of ideas makes one suspect that already before the crisis had begun to doubt such convictions; In fact, it had explicitly expressed doubts about the effectiveness of market mechanisms when, years before the crisis, it supported state intervention in the meat market. Also, in the 1931 rediscount authorization project, and very emphatically in 1932, the mechanism of asset 'liquidation' was re-chained to improve the economy and regain growth; The State cannot be liquidated and sees no advantage in liquidating the rural producer who cannot pay his credits because of the decrease in the international prices of his products". [(19)]

It was an advance in its heterodoxy, but it lacked an additional and decisive step in the implementation of active policies to remove the Argentine economy from the recession, and decide to what extent that would require the establishment of a new pattern of development, now that He was aware that the primary exporter would not, at least for a long time, play the dynamic role he had had before the crisis. That step begins to give it in the Plan of National Economic Action that elaborates with several collaborators at the end of 1933 with the explicit purpose of "to relieve the country of the weight of the economic depression". Having ordered the monetary and fiscal situation, the Plan targets a first set of measures to attack the imbalance of the balance of payments suffered by Argen-

---

(19) Adolfo Gurrieri, *Las ideas del joven Prebisch [The ideas of the young Prebisch]*, en **Revista de la CEPAL** [In **ECLAC Magazine**], N° 75, LC/G. 2150-P; pp. 76-77; Santiago de Chile, diciembre [December] 2001.

tina as an agrarian-exporting and debtor country, through devaluation and control of exchange and imports. In defense of such measures, it breaks with the scheme of the gold standard that only serves to balance alterations of the prices and the balance of payments caused by an excessive increase of the circulating one, but in 1933 these alterations had been caused by a fall of the prices of an impressive and unpredictable magnitude. Applying the gold standard mechanism, ignoring the causal importance of external factors, would deepen the crisis by provoking a huge liquidation of assets. These ideas had already formulated them before but in this Plan it emphasizes that, besides seeking the balance of the external sector, these measures had the additional objective of reactivating the economy; Exchange control and imports would protect domestic industrial activity from external competition and devaluation would benefit rural producers. Without devaluation, domestic prices of agricultural products would have fallen alongside international prices, leading to a chain-of-asset liquidation of enormous magnitude; the devaluation mitigated the impact of the decline in international prices on producers. A second set of measures was intended to boost the reactivation of industrial production through the recovery of domestic demand. Through a public works plan the government reduced unemployment and increased the purchasing power and consumption of the population, stimulating the reactivation of domestic industrial production, additionally protected by the inability to import. The protection provided by tariffs and the higher cost of foreign exchange favored consumption and domestic production, leading to a process of great importance: local industries were able to expand their production while foreign trade declined. In short, the stimulus that the Argentine economy would imperiously require could come from outside, solutions would have to come from within, from the country itself.[20]

---

(20) Adolfo Gurrieri, Ob., cit. p. 78.

It is evident, therefore, that the intense ideological struggle with the main hegemonic center begins with the Great Depression of 1929-30 and its profound repercussion on the Argentine economy, forcing Prebisch to throw away neoclassical theories, of which had nurtured his university youth; the consideration that peripheral capitalism was an integral part of the world system, ordered according to the past scheme of the international division of labor and comparative advantages, was the starting point. The capitalism of the advanced countries was essentially centripetal, and its dynamics were not enough for the periphery to promote its own development by breaking that past scheme. To achieve this goal the periphery had to be industrialized. Hence the decision to promote industrialization against the economic interests of the center as the only valid path of the underdeveloped countries is at the root of this acute ideological struggle.

3. THE CREATION OF ECLAC IN 1948 AND ITS ATTEMPT TO ELIMINATE IT IN 1951.

"My entry into the United Nations Economic Commission for Latin America in 1949 occurred," says Prebisch, "when my ideas were reaching maturity, so that I could crystallize them in several studies published in the early fifties, where I tried to present a diagnosis of the problems and the policy suggestions that would serve as options of the proposals by the Orthodox school. Thanks to the broader horizon allowed by my new responsibilities, these studies applied not only to Argentina but to Latin America as a whole".[21]

---

(21) Raúl Prebisch, *Cinco etapas de mi pensamiento sobre el desarrollo [Five stages of my thinking about development]* (ensayo presentado en un seminario del Banco Mundial [Essay presented at a World Bank seminar]), en CEPAL [in ECLAC], **Raúl Prebisch: un aporte al estudio de su pensamiento [a contribution to the study of his thinking]**, LC/G.1461, p. 14; Santiago de Chile,

I have preferred, to avoid subtleties in the interpretation, to cite the direct testimonies of the authors themselves.

*"When ECLAC was established in 1948, I was invited to head its secretariat. I did not want to accept that honorable offer. It was then a waste of time to work in economic matters at the United Nations. In my youth I had had an opportunity to see closely the activities that were carried out in these matters in the League of Nations: an Anglo-Saxon conception of the economic problems of the world, with a very marginal and episodic interest in the peripheral countries of the economy world. I was trying to explain the problems of the underdeveloped world in those days, and I supposed that in an international institution dominated by the economists of the great industrial centers it would be impossible to approach these problems with the mind free of doctrinal prejudices; shortly after I could verify my error. After having refused to accept the responsibility being offered to me, I was invited to write the introduction of the first annual Economic Survey to be presented by ECLAC to its Member Governments. It was at the beginning of 1949. The Argentine government of those times had made it impossible for me to continue in my university chair, after having been evicted from the Central Bank in whose organization I lost my better years of youth. Therefore, the invitation to move for a few months to Santiago de Chile - fortunate of the institution that had begun - had unexpected compliments to me. There, then, I wrote my first work in ECLAC on Latin American economic development .**.

---

marzo de [March] 1987. Publicación de las Naciones Unidas [Publications of the United Nations], N° de venta [Sale No] S.87.II.G.6.

* Véase *El desarrollo económico de América Latina y algunos de sus principales problemas* [See *Economic Development in Latin America and some of its main problems]* (E/CN.12/89). Se ha reproducido después en el *Boletín Económico de América Latina* [It has been reproduced later in the *Latin American Economic Bulletin*], vol. [volume] VII, N° 1, Santiago de Chile, febrero de [February] 1962, pp. 1 y [and] ss

Among other things, I proposed to demonstrate the inescapable necessity of industrialization in the economic development of the region and for the first time presented in written form my incipient ideas on the external strangulation and the deterioration in the relation of exchange prices. He was not improvising by the way. I had been exposing these ideas at the University in Buenos Aires, but I had not had the opportunity to write about them. Now that opportunity presented itself to me and I spent four unforgettable weeks writing quietly. After the task was completed, the results were sent to the United Nations headquarters in New York, long wire back. In short, it was a serious work, but too personal ideas. There was, moreover, a certain reluctance to discuss economic development. This was not precisely the objective of ECLAC. On the other hand, this insistence on Latin American industrialization could provoke unfavorable reactions. All in all, it was a good job. Why, then, does not the author sign it, submitting it under his own responsibility, without compromising the United Nations secretariat? This was, if I remember correctly - my memory is not always good - the episode of my first signing at the beginning of my adventure in ECLAC [...] This episode has something important in the life of our institution, because the fears that were harbored At the United Nations headquarters about the impact of my work, although unfounded, were not at all. Indeed, at the second meeting of ECLAC, held in Havana in mid-1949, the thesis that I held aroused great interest in Latin American countries, a strong enough interest to dominate the hostility that was already beginning to manifest itself in certain sectors. Indeed, the ideas exposed there openly challenged the dominant orthodoxy in the thinking of large industrial centers about the economic development of peripheral countries. Doctrinal critics began to emerge, most of who did not take the pain of reading our pages. They had heard something or knew some loose paragraphs. ECLAC was born in this way under the heretical sign that always presided over *its destinies. Because it was a great surprise to me - a pleasant intellectual surprise - that, after this episode, I was invited back to join the Commission. I accepted for a year to direct his studies, on the condition that my works would be subject to my own responsibility, without needing to refer me to any superior authority. This condition was accepted and was strictly enforced. What was wanted was precisely that Latin Americans would approach our problems with our own criteria, without any doctrinal support. After that first manifestation of perplexity, the men who had been leading the affairs at the United Nations headquarters had understood that this was a peremptory demand of the Latin American moment and that, if it were not answered, ECLAC would be transformed in an inconsequential bureaucratic creation. I was granted absolute freedom of action and, after that first year of experience, I did not hesitate to stay permanently at the insistent request of the central authorities. The task that had begun had finally drawn me deeply. I was offered a long horizon of research and analysis, the development of new ideas, an international institution of enlightened leadership and shelter from political arbitrariness or the influence of spurious interests that both disturb and destroy in our countries. **Staying definitively is one way of saying it, because ECLAC was created experimentally for three years, and in 1951, when the fulfillment of this period was in sight, very powerful forces came to be aimed at its elimination from the Latin American field. I knew this very well when I accepted the responsibility I was given. I had been crudely told by an eminent Latin American very in tune with the ideas prevailing there in those times. "You are wasting your time," he said to me, "because the OAS is already doing what has been entrusted to ECLAC." I do not think I lost it. The final battle was fought at our fourth session, held in Mexico in mid-1951.** It was about to become a defeat.***

**[...]"Un año antes, si mal no recuerdo, -subraya Prebisch a pregunta de Magariños- se había creado el Consejo Interamericano Económico y Social, el CIES,

Chile, which had fought enthusiastically for the creation of ECLAC, was almost isolated. Two facts were decisive at the time: (a) the position of Brazil, which after some initial hesitation took the defense of ECLAC vigorously, after its delegation, received a personal wire from President Vargas, and b) the resolute attitude of Mexico. Together with Chile, these two countries organized the resistance to bring about a total change. *A few weeks later I went to greet President Vargas in Rio, accompanied by Celso Furtado. I have rarely had such a precise and categorical dialogue in my life. In a few words, the President expressed the reason for his attitude: the need for an independent body in Latin American hands. There were in these matters around the Brazilian President a group of young economists whom I did not know and with whom I then began an invaluable friendship. Roberto Campos, Cleanto de Paiva Leite, Romulo de Almeida and Miguel de Osorio de Almeida. I suspect they had some intervention in all this. The case of Mexico was somewhat dramatic. He was Treasury Secretary Mr. Antonio Carrillo Flores, who had honored me with his longtime friendship. He invited me one night*

---

bajo la égida de la Organización del los Estados Americanos. En seguida se estableció el conflicto. Los Estados Unidos, por supuesto, nunca vieron con buenos ojos lo que se llamó la 'duplicación', y les preocupó enormemente que pudiera crearse un organismo que se sustrajera a su influencia. Mis primeros dos informes fueron la prueba clarísima del acierto de los Estados Unidos. No sólo no tuvieron el control de una Secretaría, sino que tampoco lo podían ejercer desde la sede, porque seguramente conocían la libertad de acción con que yo entré a la CEPAL [**[...] "A year ago, if I remember correctly," Prebisch points out to Magariños, "the Inter-American Economic and Social Council, CIES, under the aegis of the Organization of American States, was created. The United States, of course, never looked favorably on what was called 'duplication', and was greatly concerned that an organism could be created to extricate itself from its influence. My first two reports were the most clear proof of the success of The United States, not only did they not have control of a Secretariat, but also could not exercise it from headquarters, because they surely knew the freedom of action with which I entered ECLAC"]". (Magariños Mateos, **Diálogos con [Dialogues with] Raúl Prebisch ((testimonios [testimonies]))**, Banco Nacional de Comercio Exterior y Fondo de Cultura Económica [National Bank of Foreign Trade and Fund of Economic Culture], primera edición [first edition], p. 137; México, D.F.,1991.

*to his home to eat with Alberto Baltra and Oscar Schnake, from the Delegation of Chile, who were struggling to save and consolidate ECLAC. There was also an official - whose name I do not want to remember - who held in his hands a document. The Secretary invited him to read it after the meal. After the reading, Lic. Carrillo Flores asked the opinion of the attendees. Baltra and Schnake reacted vividly, because the text proposed the merger of ECLAC with another organism that had failed its full potential. My argument was much shorter, for that letter, which was supposed to come from the official who presented it, was exactly the same as that which, a few weeks earlier, I had categorically rejected in Washington in a similar meeting, although of a very different composition. ****

*** "Unos dos meses antes [...] indica Prebisch me invitó el embajador Dreyer a conversar, a un coctel en su casa. Fue más bien una reunión de alto nivel: había dos o tres altos funcionarios del Departamento de Estado. Y como suele hacer esta gente, fueron directamente al grano, sin preguntar por la familia, como hacemos nosotros: 'Mire, a nosotros nos preocupa mucho esta duplicación; va a ser una duplicación de esfuerzos. ¿Por qué no reunimos fuerzas? Usted sería el director de la nueva organización, que tendría todos los recursos de la CEPAL más los recursos del CIES y sería mucho más eficaz.' Y me leyeron un proyecto. Yo los escuché y luego me preguntaron qué me parecía. Les respondí: 'Miren, señores, no es el caso de ver la redacción del proyecto. Yo no estoy de acuerdo con lo fundamental, que es la fusión de las dos organizaciones. Y les voy a decir con toda claridad por qué razón. A mi juicio la significación de la CEPAL es dar a la América Latina una expresión propia y auténtica. Yo tengo esta libertad de acción. Si esto se funde, señores -no me nieguen esto- el Departamento de Estado tendría el control de la organización. Yo no digo que no sea una actitud legítima de parte de ustedes, pues son el gran poder, pero yo creo que la CEPAL significa una gran conquista de la América Latina, la de empezar a pensar con su propia cabeza, de interpretar sus problemas y las posiciones que debe de tener. Y esto no se va a poder hacer en la fusión. De manera que yo les agradezco mucho esta manifestación de confianza al hacer presente que yo sería el director de la nueva organización, pero no cuenten conmigo[...]..Y agregué: Si en un momento de debilidad yo aceptara ser el director de la nueva organización, les puedo asegurar que ninguno de los hombres que me acompañan se uniría a mí en esta fusión. Y debo agregar, y les ruego que no lo tomen a jactancia, que yo ya he cumplido cincuenta años y he mantenido una gran independencia en mi país. Si yo hubiera querido vulnerar esa independencia, seguiría todavía como gerente general del Banco Central. Y a esta altura de mi vida no estoy dispuesto a perderla. No lo

As soon as Secretary Carrillo Flores learned of these circumstances from me, he took the paper from that official, tore it violently, and threw the remains behind the sofa on which he sat. This defined the attitude of Mexico and sealed the support that this country has been unfailingly giving to ECLAC".[22]

Subsequently, an OAS meeting was held in Quitandinha, Rio de Janeiro, in 1954, known as the Quitandinha Meeting,

---

tomen ustedes a jactancia. Yo creo que tengo que ser muy franco con ustedes. Bueno, se pasó a otra cosa [...] "About two months ago", Prebisch says, "Ambassador Dreyer invited me to a cocktail party at his house. It was rather a high-level meeting: there were two or three senior State Department officials. And as these people usually do, they went straight to the point, without asking about the family, as we do: 'Look, we are very concerned about this duplication; is going to be a duplication of efforts. Why do not we gather strength? You would be the director of the new organization, which would have all the resources of ECLAC plus the resources of CIES and would be much more effective. And they read me a project. I listened to them and then they asked me what I thought. I replied: 'Look, gentlemen, it is not the case to see the draft of the project. I do not agree with the fundamental, which is the merger of the two organizations. And I will tell you very clearly why. In my opinion, the significance of ECLAC is to give Latin America its own authentic expression. I have this freedom of action. If this fuses, gentlemen - do not deny me this - the State Department would have control of the organization. I do not say that it is not a legitimate attitude on your part, because you are the great power, but I believe that ECLAC means a great conquest of Latin America, that of beginning to think with its own head, to interpret its problems and The positions that must have. And this is not going to be possible in the merger. So I thank you very much for this expression of confidence in making present that I would be the director of the new organization, but do not count on me [...] And I added: If in a moment of weakness I accept to be the director of the new organization, I can assure you that none of the men who accompany me will join me in this merger. And I must add, and I beg you, do not boast, that I am now fifty and I have maintained a great independence in my country. If I had wanted to violate that independence, I would still be the Central Bank's General Manager. And at this point in my life I am not willing to lose it. Do not take it for boasting. I think I have to be very frank with you. Well, it happened to something else"]". (Magariños Mateos, Ob., Cit. Pp. 137-138).

(22) Raúl Prebisch, **Hacia una dinámica del desarrollo latinoamericano [Towards a dynamic of Latin America development]**, Fondo de Cultura Económica [Fund of Economic Culture], primera edición [first edition], pp. VIII-X1; México D.F., 1963. Negritas de JETA [JETA Bold].

for which the Secretary of the OAS asked ECLAC for a report. Worked a group of personalities including Carlos Lleras Restrepo and Eduardo Frei Montalva, former president of Chile. The report was written by Carlos Lleras Restrepo on the basis of a basic report presented by Prebisch.

"Conscious of what that report meant," Prebisch says, "I went to see the Secretary-General Dag Hammarskjold, and I explained to him in an hour what the report contained. He said: you present it. I urged him to read it. After two days he approved it without changing a comma. Someone worried about the content of the report, since it spoke of the creation of an inter-American credit organization; of the exchange price ratio; the need to stabilize the prices of primary products; ideas such as this and others that were red-hot then. And he was very anxious to say to Hammarskjold: 'This report is going to bring us difficulties'. The Secretary-General replied: 'I have read it. Its author is skating on thin ice, but I fully support it'. This background is important because it reaffirms not only the high quality of a man and the understanding of what the United Nations means as a dynamic organism which advances economic thought beyond the rhythm imposed by current considerations, but also because this attitude fully re-affirmed the policy that from the beginning to the present day has been followed by the General Secretariat in the sense of opening new directions and encouraging new approaches to thinking in The regional economic commissions". [23]

---

(23) Raúl Prebisch, Ob., cit. p. XV. Por supuesto que los Estados Unidos recibieron muy mal el Informe. "Lo recibieron muy mal –reafirma Prebisch-. Era Humphrey - no el que fue vicepresidente sino otro-, el ministro de Hacienda, y Hoover también. Eran las cuatro haches fatídicas que tuvieron una actitud completamente negativa en Quitandinha. Años después supe por Teodoro Moscoso, que estaba en la delegación, que las instrucciones de Humphrey habían sido: *'Whenever they put a request, tell them no.'* Ésa era la instrucción general que Humphrey había dado. Fue una reunión muy agitada en la que Carlos Lleras demostró un gran talento. También estaba Felipe Herrera. La calidad de los hombres que representaban a Latinoamérica fue de primer orden. No salió nada

4. THE IMPULSE TO INDUSTRIALIZATION AND THE IDEOLOGICAL ANTAGONISM THAT PLACES ECLAC AND THE DEPARTMENT OF STATE IN THE ANTIPODE OF THE CONTRADICTION.

"It is not an undue exaggeration," says David Pollock, "to say that, in purely ideological terms, ECLAC's thinking fell like a real bomb when it first became known. In the climate at that time, it was inevitable that some US spokesmen would try to defuse it. For this reason [...] the United States had a conflictive relationship with ECLAC during the decade following its creation in 1948. The attacks against ECLAC publications were not unexpected and came from many important sectors of the American community, both from academia and from government sectors, and from the field of trade and finance. For example, American academic economists were quick to respond with a series of raids that pointed to any vulnerable point in ECLAC's theoretical armor. The attacks

---

importante, pero sí la visita del jefe de la delegación de los Estados Unidos en las Naciones Unidas, la visita a Hammarskjóld, para pedir mi cabeza: 'La delegación de los Estados Unidos no tuvo que enfrentar a la América Latina sino al señor Prebisch', dijo. Y Hammarskjóld respondió: 'He leído su informe y lo apoyo completamente.' Y terminó el asunto [Of course, the United States received the Report very badly. "They received it very badly", Prebisch says. "It was Humphrey - not the vice president but the other one - the finance minister, and Hoover as well. They were the four fateful haches who had a completely negative attitude in Quitandinha. Years later I learned from Teodoro Moscoso, who was in the delegation; that Humphrey's instructions had been: *'Whenever they put a request, tell them no'*. That was the general instruction that Humphrey had given. It was a very hectic meeting in which Carlos Lleras showed great talent. There was Felipe Herrera. The quality of the men who represented Latin America was of the first order. There was nothing important, but the visit of the head of the United States delegation to the United Nations, the visit to Hammarskjold, to ask for my head: 'The delegation of the United States did not have to face Latin America, but Mr. Prebisch himself", he said. And Hammarskjold replied: 'I have read your report and I fully support it'. And the matter was finished]". (Magariños Mateos, Ob., Cit., P 143)

were directed against various elements of his thought; However, some of them seemed to concentrate the critical attention of most American scholars, namely: dividing the world into a center-periphery dichotomy based essentially on the composition of products of international trade flows; The structuralist-monetarist approaches to the causes and remedies of inflation; Import substitution and industrialization as a priority path to overcome external constraints (balance of payments) and to absorb the unemployed and underemployed labor force; And the inadequacy of traditional trade theory, based on comparative advantages, to serve as a theoretical key to a new international division of labor. However important and important the consideration of the points enumerated above, the main target was undoubtedly Prebisch's explanation of the factors that tended to induce a secular deterioration in the relation of exchange prices between countries exporting primary products and Importers of manufactured goods". [24]

It is clear that relations between the Eisenhower administration and ECLAC became increasingly difficult during the 1950s; At the end of the decade, however, a combination of circumstances produced a change in US economic policy: President Kubitschek's recommendations for a Pan American Operation, the second report by Milton Eisenhower, brother

---

(24) David Pollock, *La actitud de los Estados Unidos hacia la CEPAL [The United States' attitude towards ECLAC] (Algunos cambios durante los últimos 30 años [Some changes over the past 30 years]);* en **Revista de la CEPAL** [in **ECLAC Magazine**]; p. 67; Santiago de Chile, Segundo semestre de [Second half of] 1978. David Pollock, de origen canadiense of Canadian origin], se incorpora a la CEPAL en los años cincuenta [joined ECLAC in the 1950's]. Fue director en la Oficina de la CEPAL en Washington, y además prestó sus servicios en México y Chile, y colaboró estrechamente durante algunos años con el Secretario General de la UNCTAD, en Ginebra [He was a director at the ECLAC Office in Washington and also served in Mexico and Chile, and worked closely with the UNCTAD Secretary-General in Geneva for some years].

of the President .*, the creation of the Inter-American Development Bank, In 1959; the economic development program approved at the Bogota Conference in 1960 and the creation of the Alliance for Progress in 1961. In a speech to the White House following his election in 1960, President Kennedy proposed that the United States and Latin America make an Alliance for Progress. Two of the elements of this bold new initiative were of particular interest: one, the goal itself, that is, to bring Latin America within a decade to a point where its economic growth could stand on its own. The other, to achieve that objective, through the collaboration of the inter-American system. ECLAC should actively engage in this process. In fact, the Alliance endorsed many ideas that had been proposed by ECLAC since 1948. Professor Arthur Schlesinger Jr., one of the architects of the Alliance, maintained that [...] "the Alliance for Progress was essentially a Latin American product, which emerged from Raúl Prebisch of Argentina and the Economic Commission for Latin America, United Nations".[25]

---

* Publicado más tarde con el título [Published later with the title] **The Wine is Bitter: The United States and Latín America (El vino amargo: Estados Unidos y América Latina**), Doubleday, New York. 1963.

(25) Arthur Schlesínger Jr., *The Alliance for Progress: A Retrospectíve*, en R. Hellman y H.J. Rosenbaum (ed.), **Latín America: The Search for a New International Role**, Halstead Press, 1974, p. 163. El profesor [Professor] L.A. Rodríguez, en un artículo titulado [in an article titled] *Experience in International Cooperation and Development*, publicado en [Published in] Growth and Change, Universidad de [University of] Kentucky, abril de [April] 1970, apoya la tesis de que la Carta de Punta del Este se basaba en las mismas recomendaciones básicas de política antes expresadas en el informe de Quitandinha de la CEPAL, en [supports the thesis that the Punta del Este Charter was based on the same basic policy recommendations previously expressed in ECLAC's Quitandinha report, in] 1954. Una tesis similar proponen [A similar thesis proposes] Jerome Levinson y Juan de Onis, **The Alliance that Lost its Way** Twentieth Century Fund, 1970, p. 63; quienes afirman, al referirse al grupo especial de planificación y desarrollo creado para colaborar en la preparación de la Carta de Punta del Este, que dicho grupo "siguió básicamente las líneas trazadas por la CEPAL en Quitandinha, siete años antes [who affirm that the group "basically followed the lines drawn up by ECLAC in Quitandinha seven years before", referring to the special planning

On this occasion, for the first time, the United States and ECLAC united to achieve economic development, and for the first time since its creation, ECLAC was mentioned by name and support was given to its work. In his address to the Alliance in 1961, President Kennedy called for "[...] a very strong Inter-American Economic and Social Council, working in conjunction with the United Nations Economic Commission for Latin America and the Inter-American Development Bank Development, should bring together leading experts from the hemisphere to help each country develop its own development plans and provide a permanent review of the hemisphere's economic progress". [26]

"The doctrines of ECLAC, for years set aside by Washington officials, appeared to be suddenly accepted, and the United States government endorsed concepts such as economic planning, regional trade agreements, and international commodity conventions". [27]

While criticism of ECLAC by US academics and businessmen continued.* in general terms they seemed to be trans-

---

and development group created to collaborate in the preparation of the Punta del Este Charter]".[...]; citado por [quoted by] David Pollock, Ob. Cit., p. 73.

(26) Ibid., p. 73.

(27) Abraham F. Lowenthal, *Liberal, Radical and Bureaucratic Perspectives on US-Latin American Policy: The Alliance for Progres in Retrospect*; en [in] Julio Cotler y Richar Fagen (ed.), **Latin America and the US: The Changing Political Realities**, Stanford Press, 1974. p. 213.

*Así, por ejemplo [Thus, for example], el [the] *Wall Street Journal* (6 de junio de [June 6] 1963) sostenía que "las ideas del señor Prebisch no merecerían mayor atención si no fuere porque conforman también la doctrina básica de la tan pregonada Alianza para el Progreso del Presidente Kennedy. De hecho, el señor Prebisch es el padrino intelectual de la Alianza. Sin embargo, los métodos propuestos por el señor Prebisch son, para muchos economistas, alternativas poco convenientes[...] Algunos expertos creen de hecho que la Alianza no logrará despegar mientras mantenga su supersticiosa creencia en la planificación gubernamental y en la asistencia estadounidense [...] La evidente falta de apoyo por parte

formed into a more conventional intellectual dispute, which was increasingly focused on aspects of statistical and analytical rigor, and away from the Ideological aspect. This period was characterized by the beginning of a series of articles much more favorable to the theses of ECLAC. .**.

---

de aquellos pocos acaudalados que disponen de recursos de inversión es tal vez uno de los mayores inconvenientes del programa económico del señor Prebisch. Meses más tarde, el mismo *Wall Street Journal* (en su editorial de 16 de octubre de 1963) afirmaba que [...]"otro aspecto de esta confusión del reformismo consiste en insistir en que las naciones latinoamericanas tracen grandes planes económicos[...]..como si nuestra propia riqueza fuera el resultado de la planificación estatal. Naturalmente, esto fomenta las tendencias socialistas que ya abundan en la región (latinoamericana) [He maintained that "the ideas of Mr. Prebisch would not deserve more attention if not because they also conform the basic doctrine of President Kennedy's much-touted Alliance for Progress. In fact, Mr. Prebisch is the intellectual godfather of the Alliance. However, the methods proposed by Mr. Prebisch are, for many economists, inconvenient alternatives [...] Some experts believe in fact that the Alliance will not be able to take off as long as it maintains its superstitious belief in governmental planning and American assistance [...] The obvious lack of support on the part of those few wealthy who have investment resources is perhaps one of the major drawbacks of Mr. Prebisch's economic program. Months later, the same Wall Street Journal (in its editorial of October 16, 1963) stated that [...] "Another aspect of this confusion of reformism is to insist that the Latin American nations draw great economic plans [...].. As if our own wealth was the result of state planning. Naturally, this fosters the socialist tendencies that already abound in the (Latin American) region]. Véase [See] David Pollock, Ob., cit. p. 75.

Es el caso de [This is the case of] Werner Baer, *The Economics of Prebisch and ECLA*, en [in] **Economic Development and Cultural Change, Vol. [Volume] X. N° 82, enero de [January] 1962; Charles A. Frankenhoff, *The Prebisch Thesis: A Theory of Industrialism for Latin America*, en [in] **Journal of inter-American Economic Studies**, Vol. [Volume] IV, N° 2, abril de [April] 1962; y especialmente en los artículos de [and especially in the articles of] Albert Hirschman, Joseph Grunwald y [and] David Félix en [in] Albert O. Hirschman (ed.) **Controversia sobre Latinoamérica [Controversy over Latin America], ensayos y comentarios [Essays and comments]**, traducción del Centro de Investigaciones Económicas [Translation of the Center for Economic Research]; Editorial del Instituto Torcuato di Tella [Editorial from the Torcuato di Tella Institute], Buenos Aires, 1963 (la edición inglesa original es de [The original English edition is from] 1961). El trabajo del profesor Hirschman titulado [The work of Professor Hirschman entitled] **Ideologías de desarrollo económico en América Latina [Ideologies of economic development in Latin America]** (y

It should be noted that ECLAC's partial honeymoon with the Government of the United States was short-lived. A few years after the Alliance for Progress, particularly with the assassination of President Kennedy in November 1963, a new stage began, during which the United States did not oppose ECLAC but did not support it, rather it could be said that They did not take it into account, of benign disinterest. Two comprehensive reviews from the points of view of the United States and Latin America, according to David Pollock, are the work of Levinson and Onis, *The Alliance that Lost its Way*, and an article by Chile's former president Eduardo Frei Montalva, also entitled *The Alliance that Lost its Way*, published in Foreign Affair, April 1967. A new stage appears to emerge, characterized by a cautious reconsideration by the United States of what is perceived as a "new ECLAC". The first visit by a Secretary of State of the United States, in this case Secretary Kissinger, to the ECLAC headquarters in Santiago, Chile, and then an informal working lunch with the Secretary Executive, Mr. Enrique Iglesias and his main collaborators. Finally, during the 30th anniversary of ECLAC, which took place in June 1978, Secretary of State Cyrus Vance congratulated, on behalf of President Carter, the Executive Secretary and the entire organization for having "contributed significantly to the vision even changing the new international economic order and development with equity and justice" [...] adding that in the "United States Government we want to support and work closely with your efforts" [...] On that same occasion, Ambassador Andrew Young expressed: "I want you to know that [...] I will spare no effort to cooperate with you and the ECLAC community in promoting their goals, because I know that you

---

en especial el capítulo sobre [and in particular the chapter on] *La situación actual y la posición dirigente de la CEPAL [The current situation and the leading position of ECLAC]*) es particularmente expresivo en este sentido [its particularly expressive in this regard]. Véase a [See] David Pollock, Ob., cit., pp. 74-75.

are committed to spreading freedom and government according to law, social justice and economic development[...]". [28]

In short, according to David Pollock, relations between the United States and ECLAC in the first 30 years of its existence can be grouped into five periods. A first period of strong suspicion by the United States about a possible duplication of OAS functions. Fearing that the new United Nations regional economic commission could challenge its dominant role within the OAS, the United States opposed the creation of ECLAC from the outset. In short, the conditions of what would soon become an increasingly marked relationship of confrontation had been traced. During the ten that followed (1948 - 1958), its second period, reserves became an open and continuous opposition. A third period (1959 - 1963), just before and during the Kennedy administration, characterized by a fundamental shift: "the United States gave ECLAC, if not a hug, at least a handshake". The fourth period (1963 - 1973) of "kind indifference" or "benevolent disinterest" comes after the assassination of President Kennedy. And, a fifth period (1973 - 1978) of "cautious revaluation" by the United States of what is perceived as a "new ECLAC".

It should be reiterated, however, that Prebisch's ideological struggle with the main hegemonic center began long before ECLAC, with the great depression of 1929 - 30 that marked its total rupture with the neoclassical school and its resolute policy of industrialization.

---

(28) David Pollock, Ob. Cit., p. 24 y ss.

IV. THE IMPORTANCE OF "STYLE", "MODEL" OR "PERIOD OF EXPANSION OR OUTWARD DEVELOPMENT" IN THE HISTORY OF UNDERDEVELOPMENT

1. THE DEFINITION OF THE "STYLE", "MODEL" OR "PERIOD OF EXPANSION OR OUTWARD DEVELOPMENT" AS A STRUCTURE, AS RELATIONSHIPS OF PRODUCTION CONCERNING THE "CENTRO-PERIPHERAL SYSTEM"

It should be reiterated that *the period, style or model of expansion or outward development*, as used here, ranges from the Industrial Revolution to the process of integration of the world economy and the new international division of labor, until the beginning of the *process of import substitution* that begins with the first World War for the most advanced countries of the region (Argentina, Brazil and Mexico). In this same sense Raúl Prebisch uses it.[1] It is important to

____

(1) "En el largo período que transcurre desde la Revolución Industrial hasta la primera Guera Mundial, la nuevas formas de producir en que la técnica ha venido manifestándose incesantemente sólo han abarcado una proporción reducida de la población mundial. [In the long period from the Industrial Revolution to the first World War, new forms of production in which technology has been unceasingly manifested only a small proportion of the world's population]. (Raúl Prebisch, *[Growth, imbalance and disparities: interpretation of the process of economic development]* (Primera parte del Estudio Económico de la América Latina [First part of the Economic Survey of Latin America], 1949, CEPAL [ECLAC]); tomado de la **Lectura** [Taken from the **Readings**] N° 46*, **La obra de Prebisch en**

emphasize this because for Cardoso this period includes the second half of the nineteenth century.

"In fact", says the author, "previous studies allow us to believe that in the phase of constitution of the National States and in the later period, *in the second half of the nineteenth century, in the phase that economists call 'outward development'"[...]*[(2)]

Likewise, we do not share the opinion of Celso Furtado.

"A SERIES of studies carried out in the last decade [1960] allow a considerable expansion of the debate on the fundamental problems of the Brazilian economy. It is becoming increasingly clear that generalities about underdevelopment, and even about the 'Latin American mold', are only a first approximation to address a historical process of characteristics as peculiar as the Brazilian. Having emphasized the specificity of underdevelopment and, in particular, the impropriety of 'phraseological' approaches that tend to transform it into a stage to be achieved in order to achieve development, emphasis was placed on the need to develop economies typologies underdeveloped, which requires a more complete knowledge of the history of the countries in which the phenomenon of underdevelopment manifests itself. **As these studies progress,**

---

la **CEPAL** [Prebisch's work at ECLAC], Selección de [Selection of] Adolfo Gurrieri en dos partes [in two parts], de la serie Lecturas de El Trimestre Económico [Of the Series of the Economic Quarter]; Fondo de Cultura Económica [Fund of Economic Culture], primera edición [first edition]; Primera parte [First part] (El programa inicial en la CEPAL [The initial program in ECLAC]), p. 156; México, 1982.

(2) Fernando H. Cardoso, **Ideologías de la burguesía industrial en sociedades dependientes [Ideologies of the industrial bourgeoisie in dependent societies] (Argentina y Brasil [Argentina and Brazil]);** Siglo veintiuno editores [21st century publishers]; segunda edición en español [second edition in Spanish], p. 63; México D.F., 1972.

it becomes more evident that the analytical models with which the underdevelopment theorist has worked, such as the 'development out' and the 'import substitution', are of limited scope interpretative. Perhaps one of the most serious limitations that can be blamed on these models is that they were built without adequate knowledge of certain structures, particularly agrarian structures. That observation is valid, no doubt, in the case of Brazil".[3]

This opinion of Furtado, valid for the case of the **agrarian** structures in Brazil, is not when it comes to characterizing the specific and dominant structures in underdevelopment. And in this sense, *period, style or model of expansion or 'outward development'; or 'import substitution'* model or style are common to Brazil and to any other underdeveloped country.

On the other hand, the concepts of "styles" or "development models" are being used, as Jorge Glaciarena does, to refer to the concept of "system" and "structure"[4]; Or to say

---

(3) Celso Furtado, **El subdesarrollo latinoamericano [Latin America underdevelopment]**; Fondo de Cultura Económica [Fund of Economic Culture], primera edición en español [first edition in Spanish], p. 27; México, 1982. Negritas de JETA [JETA Bold].

(4) Jorge Graciarena, *Poder y estilo de desarrollo: una perspectiva heterodoxa [Power and style of development: a heterodox perspective* (publicado en la **Revista de la CEPAL** [Published in the **ECLAC Review**], **N° 1**, Santiago de Chile, CEPAL, p. 678; primer semestre de 1976. Publicación de las Naciones Unidas, N° de venta: S.76.II.G.2. "Cuando se usó la palabra estilos –apunta el autor- no pocos creyeron que se cerraba una etapa en el proceso de ensayo y error del pensamiento sobre el desarrollo basado en posiciones valorativas e ideológicas y en una terminología obsoleta, y que se abría hacia el futuro una ancha y promisoria avenida. No ha sido así, y viejos problemas se vaciaron en un nuevo molde sin que eso significara otra cosa que un cambio nominal. Cuando se mencionan los estilos (o modelos) de desarrollo en seguida se suscitan varias preguntas fundamentales: ¿Cuál es su sentido, o sea a qué cosa de la realidad se refiere este concepto? ¿En qué posición del campo teórico sobre los procesos de desarrollo se inserta? ¿Cuáles son sus elementos fundamentales y secundarios, y qué clase de relaciones hay entre ellos? [...] ¿cuál es el método más adecuado para tratar con

it with Anibal Pinto, "I coincide almost entirely with one of
the definitions proposed by J. Graciarena, according to which

---

los problemas que involucra? Las preguntas no terminan aquí, pero las indicadas bastan para señalar las direcciones principales de nuestras dificultades cuando se examinan los varios documentos y trabajos emanados del proyecto sobre el enfoque unificado[...] Un problema no menos importante pero naturalmente más formal –agrega en otro lugar- es el del *nivel de análisis*. Hay bastante confusión en la posición metodológica subyacente en la idea de estilo, pues según se mostró páginas atrás, el concepto alude con frecuencia a situaciones potenciales o concretas de muy diverso rango. Así sucede, por ejemplo, cuando se habla de un estilo 'mundial', de otro 'nacional', para referirse finalmente a situaciones de alcance más limitado que corresponden al orden de las estrategias circunstanciales. De esta manera el estilo aparece a veces como un sucedáneo de sistema (capitalista, socialista), de estructura o de régimen; en otras ocasiones, en cambio, sería algo parecido a una fase en el proceso de desarrollo, como cuando se habla de desarrollo hacia fuera', de 'sustitución de importaciones' o de 'internacionalización del mercado', que podrían ser (y han sido) señalados como estilos prevalecientes de desarrollo (económico y político) ["When the word 'style' was used, the author points out, not a few believed that a stage was closed in the process of trial and error of development thinking based on values and ideological positions and an outdated terminology that opened to the future a wide and promising avenue. It has not been so, and old problems were emptied into a new mold without that meant anything other than a nominal change. When one mentions the development styles (or models), then several fundamental questions arise: What is its meaning, or what is the meaning of this concept? In what position of the theoretical field on development processes is inserted? What are their fundamental and secondary elements, and what kind of relationships are there between them? [...] What is the most appropriate method to deal with the problems involved? The questions do not end here, but those indicated are enough to point out the main directions of our difficulties when examining the various documents and papers emanating from the project on the unified approach [...] An issue no less important but naturally more formal, he adds elsewhere, is the level of analysis. There is a great deal of confusion in the methodological position underlying the idea of style, for as we have seen pages back, the concept often refers to potential or concrete situations of very different rank. This is the case, for example, when one speaks of a 'world', a 'national' style, to refer finally to situations of more limited scope corresponding to the order of circumstantial strategies. In this way, style sometimes appears as a substitute for system (capitalist, socialist), structure or regime; On other occasions, it would be something like a phase in the development process, such as when one speaks of 'outward development', 'import substitution' or 'internationalization of the market', which could be (and have been) designated as prevailing styles of development (economic and political)]". (Ibid., p. 665-666 y 678).

style would be 'the concrete and dynamic modality adopted by a system in a defined area and in a determined historical moment'".[5] I also agree with his appreciation that the "proposition refers rather to a structure than to a style", provided that by structure we understand the relations of production and not a social formation. It is worth emphasizing that in this point Anibal Pinto differs from Jorge Graciarena.

[...] "I do not agree with his appreciation", says Pinto, "that this proposition refers more to a structure (or to a social formation) than to a style". For me, its reference to the 'sphere' must be understood precisely as a consideration of the structural fact of the 'developed-underdeveloped' complex referred to above".[6]

In sum, the concepts of **styles** or **models** are used here as *structures*, as *relations of production* referred to the **"center-periphery system"**, and specifically the three phases with different structures of the evolution of underdevelopment: 1) the **"period", "Style" or "outward development model"**; (2) the **"period", "style" or "inward development model" or "import substitution model"**; and (3) the **"period", "style" or "internationalization model of the internal market"**; three **"structures"** other than the **"center-periphery system"**.

In the first of these phases the specific social classes of underdevelopment arise and develop; hence its historical importance.

---

(5) Anibal Pinto, *Notas sobre estilos de desarrollo [Notes on development styles]: origen, naturaleza y esquema conceptual [Origin, nature and conceptual scheme]*; en **Revista Paraguaya de Sociología** [In **Paraguayan Journal of Sociology**]; Año [Year] 29, N° 84; p. 597; mayo-agosto de [May-August] 1992.

(6) Anibal Pinto, Ob.cit. p. 597.

It is, therefore, our task now to deal with the theoretical question of the problem, that is, to explain from the point of view of Political Economy, where do the specific social classes of underdevelopment arise and what do their characteristic features consist of? The correct answer to these questions will allow us to understand why the capitalist system did not follow Marx's path of development in the peripheral economies.[7] The problem has not been attacked by any author and advances in the study of the social classes specific to the phenomenon have been limited to historical verification regardless of the etiology of their real nature. It is not by chance, therefore, that Cardoso and Faletto have insisted on the approach of the problem.

*"The recognition of the historicity of the situation of underdevelopment," they emphasize, "requires more than pointing out the structural characteristics of underdeveloped economies. It is necessary to analyze, in effect, how the under-developed economies are historically linked to the world market and **the way in which the social groups** (it must have been mentioned the social classes) **were constituted that managed to define the outward relationships that underdevelopment supposes".**[8]*

---

(7) Marx sostenía que [Marx maintained that], "los países industrialmente más desarrollados no hacen más que poner delante de los países menos progresivos el espejo de su propio porvenir [The industrially most developed countries do nothing more than put before the less progressive countries the mirror of their own future]" (C. Marx, **El Capital [The Capital]**, Tomo [Volume] I, Ediciones Venceremos [Overcome Editions], La Habana [Havana], 1965, p. XXII).

(8) Fernando Henrique Cardoso y [and] Enzo Faletto, **Dependencia y Desarrollo en América Latina [Dependence and Development in Latin America]**, Siglo XXI [21st Century], ed. 2a.; pp. 23-24; México, 1970. Cursivas de JETA [JETA Italics].

Let us see, then, what are the theoretical-historical premises that explain the emergence of the specific social classes of underdevelopment.

2. THE THEORETICAL-HISTORICAL PREMISES THAT EXPLAIN THE APPEARANCE OF THE SOCIAL CLASSES SPECIFIC TO UNDERDEVELOPMENT.

The integration of the world economy and the emergence of what I have called the **monoproduction**,[9] as a peculiar system of social production profoundly disrupted the virtual

---

(9) El concepto **monoproducción** se utiliza aquí, con el mismo sentido que las Naciones Unidas emplean la expresión "concentración de las exportaciones en un número pequeño de productos primarios". Se trata, pues, de caracterizar con este concepto **no tanto** la producción o exportación de un solo producto, como la **tendencia histórico-natural** de los países subdesarrollados a mantenerse como **apéndice** de los grandes centros industriales, o para ser más exactos, como productores de un número reducido de productos primarios para el mercado mundial. Sólo en este sentido son **monoproductores. Nos referimos, por tanto, a la producción de productos primarios para el mercado mundial y no para el mercado interno**, es decir, a la situación que le asigna a estos países la nueva división internacional del trabajo que implanta la Revolución Industrial al integrarse la economía mundial. Importa subrayarlo porque el concepto **monoproducción** en su sentido literal significa producción de un solo producto. Lo que, por otra parte, no quiere decir, de ninguna manera que no existan formas puras de monoproducción. En **1957**, por ejemplo, el azúcar constituía el **99%** del valor de las exportaciones de la Isla Mauricio; en **1958**, del valor total de las exportaciones, al petróleo le correspondía el **99%** en las Antillas Neerlandesas, el **92%** en Irak y el **91%** en Venezuela [The **monoproduction** concept is used here, with the same meaning as the United Nations uses the expression "concentration of exports in a small number of primary products". It is therefore a question of characterizing with this concept **not so much** the production or exportation of a single product, as the **historical-natural tendency** of underdeveloped countries to maintain themselves as an **appendage** of the great industrial centers, or, to be more exact, producers of a limited number of primary products for the world market. Only in this sense are **mono-producers. We refer, therefore, to the production of primary products for the world market and not**

conditions for the normal development of capitalism on the periphery. The linkage of these economies to the world market, particularly to the English market, which imposed the new international division of labor, inevitably led, in this part of the world, to the **independent** development of capital at the extremes of production, that is, the **autonomous** development of Commercial capital and industrial capital. The absolutism of capital at its extremes is the theoretical basis that explains, on the one hand, the emergence and evolution of the specific classes of underdevelopment, its characteristic features, and, on the other hand, atrophy and deformed capitalism on the periphery.

---

for the domestic market, that is to say, the situation that these countries assign to the new international division of labor that implants the Industrial Revolution when integrating the economy world. It should be emphasized that the concept of **monoproduction** in its literal sense means production of a single product. What, on the other hand, does not mean, in any way that there are no pure forms of monoproduction. In **1957**, for example, sugar constituted **99%** of the value of exports from Mauritius; in **1958**, of the total value of exports, oil accounted for **99%** in the Netherlands West Indies, **92%** in Iraq and **91%** in Venezuela]. Véase "Convenios Internacionales sobre productos básicos [See "International commodity agreements]", preparado por el profesor [prepared by professor] J. E. Meade, en *Actas de la Conferencia de las Naciones Unidas sobre Comercio y Desarrollo [In Proceedings of the United Nations Conference on Trade and Development]*, Ginebra 23 de marzo -16 de junio de [Geneva March 23th – June 16th] 1964, **Vol. [Volume] III, Intercambio de Productos [Product Exchange]** (E/CONF.46/141/ Vol. III). Como vemos, el contenido del concepto no expresa con exactitud su sentido etimológico. Es el problema de la imprecisión de las categorías que se repite en todas las ciencias cuando surgen fenómenos nuevos. Muchas veces a la ciencia no le queda más recurso que manejar conceptos y categorías que no son, por su inexactitud, los más adecuados para fijar los nuevos fenómenos. Sin embargo, el concepto monoproducción, que no escapa a esta dificultad, nos parece la categoría más apropiada para referirnos a este sujeto [As we can see, the content of the concept does not accurately express its etymological meaning. It is the problem of the imprecision of categories that is repeated in all sciences when new phenomena arise. Many times science has no other recourse than to manage concepts and categories that are not, by their inaccuracy, the most adequate to fix new phenomena. However, the monoproduction concept, which does not escape this difficulty, seems to us the most appropriate category to refer to this subject].

The independent development of commercial capital gave birth to the **importing commercial bourgeoisie**, while the autonomous development of industrial capital flourished the **export bourgeoisie**. The group of these groups that I have called the **modern oligarchy** came to be the **social expression** of the monoproductive regime, that is, of that regime that served as **communicating vessel** between the periphery and the center.

In the history and **proverbial** development of capitalism, commercial capital has played an important role. Marx has deeply analyzed in Capital the importance and function of this substantive element.

*"Within the capitalist system of production - that is, as soon as the capitalist seizes the production itself and prints out a completely new and specific form - commercial capital appears simply as capital destined to a **specific** function [...] The Commercial Capital enterprise ceases to have its own independent existence as a former to become a special aspect of capital investment in general terms, and the compensation of profits is responsible for reducing its share of profit to the general share of profit. Commercial activity simply acts as an agent of industrial capital. Now, the special social states created by the development of commercial capital are no longer a determinant factor: on the contrary, where this type of capital predominates, old-fashioned social states prevail [...] In modern English history, traders in the strict sense and commercial cities also present themselves as politically reactionary factors and allied to the landed and financial aristocracy against industrial capital. One should not look, for example, at the political role played by Liverpool against Manchester and Birmihgham. Trade capital and the moneyed interest of England did not fully recognize the hegemony of industrial capital until tariffs on wheat were abolished. The independent*

and predominant development of capital as commercial capital amounts to the non-submission of production to capital and thus to the development of capital on the basis of a social form of production alien to and independent of capital. The independent development of commercial capital is, therefore, in inverse proportion to the general economic development of society". [10]

Therefore, under the capitalist system of production, commercial capital ceases to have its own independent existence to become a mere agent of industrial capital. This set up the development of that and between both establishes a reciprocal relationship of mutual correspondence that allows the normal development of the system, that is, the sphere of production and the sphere of circulation. The harmony between these spheres guarantees the healthy and vigorous growth of the whole system.

Now the polarization of the absolute development of capital at its extremes breaks the harmony between the two spheres of production, while at the same time provoking the atrophic development of the whole system of production. Marx clearly perceives in his work the pathogenesis that goes hand in hand with the independent development of commercial capital.

*[...] "On the way commercial capital operates where production directly dominates," he tells us in a passage in **The Capital**, "we have a clear testimony not only in the colonial economy in general (in the so-called colonial system), but Especially in the economy of the former Dutch company of the East Indies".* [11]

---

(10) Carlos Marx, **El Capital [The Capital], Editorial Nacional de Cuba [National Editorial of Cuba], Vol [Volume] III**, pp. 347-348; La Habana [Havana], 1963.

(11) Carlos Marx, Ob. cit., p. 350.

"Where this type of capital predominates, old-fashioned social states prevail." Underdevelopment is precisely one of these types of antiquated social states.

It is not difficult to understand that the characteristics of the specific social classes of underdevelopment, of what I have called the **modern oligarchy**, derive from the absolute development of capital at its extremes, that is, from the independent and autonomous development of commercial capital and industrial capital.

The antiquated social states that emerge on the periphery of the capitalist system as the world economy is integrated and the new international division of labor is introduced, however, are distinguished from those antiquated social states that are characteristic of the prehistory of the capitalist production system. These differences can be summarized in the following points:

1. While in the prehistory of capital, old-fashioned social states appear as a special historical form of capital long before capital itself undergoes its own production, the existence of the backward social states of underdevelopment springs forth as soon as capital seizes the production and prints a completely new and specific form, that is, as soon as the great machinized industry established by the Industrial Revolution is established.

2. If, in the preliminary stages of capitalist evolution, outdated social states are created as a consequence of the independent and autonomous development of commercial capital, in the phase of integration of the world economy and the formation of underdevelopment, those anomalous states that arise in the periphery of the system are not only originated by the predominant development of commercial capital

but by the **late transfiguration of industrial capital**. At this point we find the autonomous and independent development of capital at its extremes, that is, with the polarization of the absolute development of commercial capital and industrial capital. Capital destroys the internal relationship between the two spheres of production and escapes the national market to link to the world market.

3. Conversely, what happened in the prehistory of capital where the independent development of commercial capital and therefore of the antiquated social states that it engendered constituted a brake on the normal evolution of capitalism, the absolute development of commercial and industrial capital and social states regressive processes that procreate in the periphery are but the **sine qua non** condition of its later development.

As a consequence of the above points, the changes in the relationship between commercial capital and the general economic development of the society discovered by Marx can be expressed in the following law. **The autonomous and independent development of commercial and industrial capital on the periphery of the capitalist system is directly due to the development of industrial capitalism in the centers and in inverse proportion to the general economic development of society.**

From all of the above, it can be inferred that the "specific" social classes of underdevelopment, **the importing commercial bourgeoisie, and the export bourgeoisie**, that is, the classes that make up what I have called the **modern oligarchy**, arise with absolute development and Independent of commercial capital and industrial capital in the periphery; That these classes are no more than the **social expression** of monoproduction, that is, of the **peculiar system of produc-**

tion that the new international division of labor implanted in the integration of the world economy. While it is true that the autonomous development of commercial capital, and hence of the commercial bourgeoisie, is already present in the prehistory of capital, it is no less certain that the finished and brutal form of this absolutization of capital is a **specific characteristic of the phase of the large machinized industry. It is there that the independent and autonomous development of capital in the periphery becomes law of the development of the center organized as an industrial production field.**

3. TOWARDS A PRECISION OF THE "OLIGARCHY" CONCEPT IN LATIN AMERICA: FROM "MODERN OLIGARCHY" TO "TRADITIONAL OLIGARCHY".

From all that we have hitherto developed, it is not difficult to analyze the successes and failures of ECLAC's theory of the period of outward expansion and the formation of the specific social classes of underdevelopment.

In Prebisch's case it is evident his success in distinguishing the **"period", "style" or "outward development model"**, the **"period", "style" or "inward development model"** or **"import substitution model"**. Here are some substantive differences.

"The differences between the type of present development and the past are very clear when comparing the characteristics of the process that happens now with the phenomena that occurred in the last century and the first decades of the present. There is, of course, no clear and neat dividing line between them. The present forms of development have begun

*long ago in some Latin American countries, driven by the dynamics of their economy, while in others they begin in more recent times. But in all of them **they were external contingencies such as the world wars and the great economic crisis, those that helped to awaken or intensify the process and progressively settle the ideas of development [...] Both types of development differ in the objective that they pursue, in the extension they take and in the way the process is fulfilled.***

While past development was primarily concerned with the primary needs of the major industrial centers, the purpose of the present one is to raise the level of consumption in the countries in which it takes place. In one case the export is the instrument to obtain all kinds of imports of manufactured products; in the other, it is the instrument to achieve the progressive development of its internal production.** In that case, modern production techniques were generally confined to activities directly or indirectly linked to exports, while in the current process technical progress sought to extend to all branches of activity to achieve this increase in Level of consumption by adapting the forms of production of the most developed countries [...] The more developed countries, by investing capital in the primary production of the least developed, did so to satisfy their own consumption more cheaply. In the development of now, on the contrary, most of the capitalization has to come out of the savings of developing countries themselves in order to raise the consumption of their masses of population. **Foreign investment, which was once the main element, now becomes an additional element, although of considerable importance. The leading groups of the past were thus exempt from the need to capitalize on export-related activities and could devote their high incomes to consumption, adopting the forms of existence of large countries; In this way the forms of culture and the refinements of European civilization gradually spread to them, with very

slow irradiation to the denser and deeper layers of popular life". *(12)*

It is true that if Prebisch ignores the analysis of the specific classes of underdevelopment here, it is no less true that he establishes a clear difference between the *style* or *model of outward expansion* and the *style* or *model of expansion inward.*

As regards the specific social classes of underdevelopment, here are the various conceptions of the modern oligarchy.

"The political history of Latin America," Cardoso points out, "has been dominated by the concept of oligarchy, a concept that precisely emphasizes the pact between the modern and the most advanced modern export sector" [...](13) *In another place remarks: [...] "The oligarchy (we repeat, the alliance between the capitalist agro-exporting groups and the landowners of low productivity) endured with great success the pressures 'from below'" [...].*(14) *"The very process of in-*

---

(12) Raúl Prebisch, *Problemas teóricos y prácticos del crecimiento económico [Theoretical and practical problems of economic growth];* tomado de la **Lectura** [Taken from **Reading] 46 (La obra de Prebisch en la CEPAL [Prebisch's work at ECLAC],** selección de [selection of] Adolfo Gurrieri en dos partes [in two partes]), de la Serie de Lecturas de El Trimestre Económico [Of the Economic Quarter Reading Series]; Fondo de Cultura Económica [Fund of Economic Culture], primera edición [first edition]; Primera parte [First part] (El programa inicial en la CEPAL [The initial program in ECLAC]); pp. 248-250; México, 1982. Negritas de R.P [R.P Bold].

(13) Fernando H. Cardoso, *"Presentación de los comentarios y discusiones de la cuarta y quinta sesiones [Presentation of the comments and discussions of the fourth and fifth sessions]",* en **Las clases sociales en América Latina** [In **Social classes in Latin America]. Problemas de conceptualización [Problem of conceptualization]** (Seminario de [Seminary of] Mérida, Yucatán) Instituto de Investigaciones Sociales, U.N.A.M. [Institute of Social Research, U.N.A.M]; coordinado por [Coordinated by] Raúl Benítez Zenteno, Siglo XXI [21ˢᵗ Century], la. Ed. p. 426, México, 1973.

(14) Fernando H. Cardoso, **Ideologías de la burguesía industrial en sociedades dependientes [Ideologies of the industrial bourgeoisie in dependent**

dependence," he argues elsewhere, "was the result of the action of the agro-exporting groups which, by breaking political ties with Portugal or Spain, maintained control of the internal productive system and reorganized their links in the international market, orienting them in the direction of the then dominant hegemonic center in the capitalist world: England".[15]

This position seems to us completely wrong. The large landowners of low productivity cannot be included in the modern oligarchy, for these classes represent feudalism, while the specific classes of underdevelopment are the daughters of modern capitalism, of the Industrial Revolution. In addition, the modern oligarchy and the large landowners of low productivity face, immediately after independence in a bloody struggle, the war between liberals and conservatives that in some countries of the region like Colombia, covers almost all the nineteenth century. They could hardly form an alliance of classes. On the other hand, Cardoso does not include in the modern oligarchy the importing commercial bourgeoisie, without which it is not possible to understand the first half of the nineteenth century, particularly Ibero-American independence. Contrary to what the author maintains, Latin American independence was not the result of the action of the agro-exporting groups, but of the struggle of the importing merchants, that is, of the importing commercial bourgeoisie for the freedom of commerce.

In his critique of Cardoso's definition, Ernest Mandel stresses:

"The traditional definition of the oligarchy as an alliance between forces of pre-capitalist, semi-capitalist, possess-

---

societies] (Argentina y Brasil [Argentina and Brazil]); Siglo XXI [21ˢᵗ Century]; 2a. Ed. p. 109; México, 1972.

(15) Ibid., p. 63.

ing classes (the author refers to agrarian-exporting groups -JETA-) and capitalists (capital-buyers) with foreign capital seems most satisfactory".[16]

However, Mandel, as we see, repeats the same mistake as Cardoso. The advance here consists of the incorporation of the commercial-import bourgeoisie in the composition of the modern oligarchy.

A different variant, with some similar points, is found in Jorge Graciarena. The fundamental ideas of this author can be summarized in the following paragraphs:

The "national export oligarchies" [...] generally correspond to the period of 'outward development' and are therefore based on the production and export of primary products[...].. The sources of power[...]..are still rural, although the landowners live in the cities".[17] The "oligarchies landowners [...] are based on the large semi-feudal agrarian property that produces for export cattle or agricultural products: this is the case of the Peruvian gamonal, the great Brazilian farmer and the Rio de la Plata farmers".[18]

The mistakes of this position are evident. In the first place, the modern oligarchy, as we have already pointed out, cannot be reduced to the exporting groups. This is only one of its

---

(16) Ernest Mandel, *Clases sociales y crisis política en América Latina [Social classes and political crisis in Latin America]*, en la Revista **Economía Política** del Instituto de Investigaciones Económicas y Sociales de la Universidad Nacional Autónoma de Honduras [in the Journal Political Economic of the Institute of Economic and Social Investigations of the National Autonomous University of Honduras], No. 12, p. 96.

(17) Jorge Graciarena, **Poder y clases sociales en el desarrollo de América Latina [Power and social classes in the development of Latin America]**, Editorial Paidos; p. 64 y 57; Buenos Aires, 1967.

(18) Ibid., p. 65.

components. It is not legitimate to exclude, under no reason, importers, i.e. the importing merchant bourgeoisie, from this concept. Therefore, the sources of power originate from an urban and rural base. Secondly, it is incorrect to argue that the exporters (such is the case of the Peruvian gamonal, the great Brazilian farmer, and the Rio de la Plata farmers) form a land owning oligarchy, although the organization of production, particularly, the relationships of production, have a semi-feudal character. The modern oligarchy that is born organically linked to monoproduction and, consequently, to the process of integration of the world market, is the daughter of modern capitalism. As such it is always a **bourgeois oligarchy**. The **bourgeois character** of this oligarchy is determined, therefore, by its congenital link with the world market and capitalist development. That is why; despite the slave relations of the cotton plantations that existed in the South of the United States, such as the **semi-feudal** relations of the plantations of the United Fruit Company, these plantations are eminently bourgeois. This problem had already been solved by Marx in the fifties of the last century.

"If today," he asserted, referring to the slave-owners of the southern United States, "we not only do we call the planters of America capitalist but they are, that is because they exist as anomalies within a world market based on free labor".[19] Hence the reason that Pinto assists him when he states: "It is clear that the sectors that appear alongside the landowning class (and that are commonly associated with it) can be called bourgeoisie".[20]

---

(19) Centro d'Etudes et de Recherches Marxistes [Center for Marxist Studies and Research], **Sur les sociétés précapitalistes [On pre-capitalist societies]**; Editions Sociales [Social Editions], p. 224; París, 1970.

(20) Aníbal Pinto Santa Cruz, **Chile un caso de desarrollo frustrado [Chile a case of frustrated development]**; Editorial Universitaria [University Publishing], pp., 38-39; Santiago de Chile, 1969.

Putting things this way, Mandel's position seems indefensible to us. Referring to the definition of Cardoso, this author points out:

"The definition of this old oligarchy as an 'agrarian bourgeoisie of exportation' and a class of territorial owners (landowners) cannot be accepted as a factor. **The fact of exporting goods to the world market, in symbiosis with imperialist, it is not enough to justify the label of capitalists.**

We must begin by defining the relations of production which have allowed the exported commodities to be produced. When these relationships of production are mixed, hybrid, and combined, we have them with a dominant class, a hybrid which itself deserves at most a semi-capitalist label".[21]

As we see Mandel abandons the conception of Marx on this point. It is important to note that Engels shared the same opinion: In 1862 he wrote:

[...] "I am [...] convinced of the bourgeois nature of the planters" [...].[22]

Some ECLAC scholars such as Celso Furtado and Osvaldo Sunkel consider it essential to distinguish what they call **feudal oligarchy (landed aristocracy, land owning class, large landowners and traditional landlords)** linked to the **urban merchant class** (the representatives of the commercial monopoly imposed by Spain in America Since the beginning of the sixteenth century) of the export-importing bourgeoi-

---

(21) Ernest Mandel, Ob. cit., p. 96. Cursivas de JETA [JETA Italics].

(22) **Oeuvres Complètes de [Complete Works of] Carl Marx**, *"Correspondance [Correspondence] K. Marx-Fr. Engels",* Colección publicada por [Collection published by] A. Babel y Ed. Berenstein, en edición de Alfred Costés [in Alfred Costés edition], Tomo [Volume] VIII, pp. 109-110; Paris, 1934.

sie that emerges from the process of integration of the world economy.

"Alongside the feudal oligarchy, which has been over-turned in the great dominions," Furtado says, "there was tra-ditionally an urban merchant class in the country. In colonial times this one was mainly constituted by Portuguese born in the metropolis. With independence, an evolution occurred. Part of the said class was linked to English interests, which at that time had control of import and export operations, and as-sumed a cosmopolitan physiognomy. Another part, preferably in the new regions, such as coffee, turned to the agricultural sector, acting as a link between the then expanding external markets and the rural sectors, which tended to isolate them-selves. In this second case, a bourgeoisie would be formed, which would not only control commercial and financial trans-actions of export and import, but would also be linked to ag-ricultural activities. This bourgeoisie was the first initiative to establish the coffee railways, to promote immigration of European origin and other similar measures". [23]

"Another new fact that introduces an important variant in the social structure of the colony" Sunkel argues, in turn, "is the emergence and / or strengthening of new groups, partic-ularly foreign importers and merchants, especially English. This is a significant element in countries that had already de-veloped, prior to emancipation, links of some importance to England, which were strengthened and expanded during the independence process and thereafter. In countries like Argen-tina and Chile, export and import trade passes largely from Creole or Spanish hands to English hands, as a consequence

---

(23) Celso Furtado, *Brasil: De la República oligárquica al Estado militar [Bra-zil: From the oligarchic republic to the military state];* en **Brasil hoy** [in **Brazil today**], Siglo veintiuno editores [Century twenty-one publishers], primera edi-ción en español [first edition in Spanish]; p. 3-4; México, 1968.

of the opening of ports, demanded by Great Britain as a condition for the recognition of the new states".[24]

This position of distinguishing what they call the **feudal oligarchy** (landed aristocracy, landowner class, large landowners and traditional landlords) linked to the **urban merchant class** (the representatives of the commercial monopoly imposed by Spain in America since the beginning of the sixteenth century) of the **bourgeoisie exporter-importer** that emerges from the process of integration of the world economy, I think it is correct and a way to contribute to the precision of the oligarchic classes in Latin America.

The lack of rigor in the use of the concept of **oligarchy** has led certain authors to deny the scientific validity of the concept and to pronounce, even for its elimination.

"As far as the analysis of the dominant classes is concerned" for example, Agustín Cuevas argues in his commentary on a paper by Torres Rivas, "I would like to suggest, finally, that the concept of 'oligarchy' should be discarded once and for all, a term which, rather than facilitating socio-political analysis, makes it difficult. In the paper itself, this concept is used to refer to at least four different situations: that of the Ecuadorian or Bolivian landed aristocracy, which in fact is not even (or was) a kind of capitalist mode of production, that of the agribusiness bourgeoisie of Guayaquil, for example, that of the mining bourgeoisie of Bolivia, that of the block in power of several countries, the only case for which it may be pertinent to retain the term. "And it is not a question" adds Cuevas "of a theoretical subtlety, but of the need to elaborate

---

(24) Osvaldo Sunkel y Pedro Paz, **El Subdesarrollo latinoamericano y la teoría del desarrollo [Latin American Underdevelopment and Development Theory]**; Siglo XXI Editores [21ˢᵗ Century Publishers], S.A., primera edición [first edition]; p. 302; México, 1970.

more precise conceptual tools that allow us to discover, for example, the class logic underlying the horrific political crisis in Ecuador in the 1930s, logic impossible to grasp if one begins by envisaging the dominant classes and fractions in the ambiguous concept of 'oligarchy'". [25]

This seems to me an inappropriate position. The author himself implicitly recognizes it in a later work entitled **The development of capitalism in Latin America** (essay of historical interpretation), 1ª. Ed .; Mexico, 1977; In which, despite the opinion expressed here, he uses the concept of "oligarchy" to refer to different situations. For example, Chapters 5, 7 and 8 are entitled "The oligarchic development dependent on capitalism", "the oligarchic state" and "the class struggle and the transformation of oligarchic society".

It is evident, therefore, that it is not through the elimination of concepts such as that of "oligarchy", so useful in the analysis of the specific social classes of underdevelopment, as we will overcome the insufficiencies of the conceptual instrument of which we have today, but through its correct and proper elaboration.

From this perspective, we agree with Torres Rivas' point of view.

---

(25) Agustín Cuevas, *Comentario a la ponencia de [Commentary to the paper by] Edelberto Torres Rivas* "Notas sobre la crisis de la dominación burguesa en América Latina [Notes on the crisis of bourgeois domination in Latin America]", en **Clases sociales y crisis política en América Latina [In Social classes and political crisis in Latin America]** (Seminario de [Seminary of] Oaxaca), organizado por el Instituto de Investigaciones Sociales de la U.N.A.M. [Organized by the Institute of Social Research of the U.N.A.M.], coordinado por [Coordinated by] Raúl Benítez Zenteno; Siglo [Century] XXI, 1a. Ed.; pp. 107-108; México, 1977.

[...] "The concept of oligarchy (with or without quotation marks) reveals itself almost as a void of historical content if its use is not previously defined and articulated to a stage of Latin American development. We talk about oligarchy thinking about the old rural bourgeoisie, the agrarian class that lived and is still invigorated by the export trade of primary products, others spoke of the old and the new oligarchy and, with some reason, some who defended the oligarchic adjective as a mere political style, as a conduct of power". [26]

Hence, the importance of the differentiation introduced by authors like Furtado, Sunkel and others, in the use of the concept **"oligarchy"**, without this differentiation it is impossible to understand the modern history of Latin America, particularly the structure and class struggle in the nineteenth century and the twentieth century. That is why in using the concept of "oligarchy"; I distinguish the **modern oligarchy** from the **traditional oligarchy**.

The serious errors that in Latin American historiography impede the understanding of our modern and contemporary history are due in great part to the lack of rigor and precision both in the analysis of these social groups and the classes that integrate them as well as the inappropriate use of the concepts and categories that designate them.

Let's look at some examples.

"Historical analysis shows", Cardoso points out, "that independence was made by the fraction of the dominant classes most closely linked to the dynamic interests of capitalism, that

---

(26) Edelberto Torres Rivas, *Historia y estructura en el Seminario de Oaxaca [History and structure in the Seminary of Oaxaca] (comentario final al seminario [Final comment to the seminar]),* en [in] Ibid. p. 392.

is, the agro-exporting group, not the landowner group".[27]
"It would be a mistake to think", Cardoso and Faletto point
out, referring to the case of Colombia, "that the conservative
liberal struggle of the nineteenth century expresses an oppo-
sition between the noble-landowners sectors on the one hand
and the bourgeois-capitalist sectors on the other".[28]

This first interpretation, as we have seen, seems to me unfortunate. Without diminishing the importance of the exporting groups, independence, in fact, was led by Creole traders
in the port cities of the Continent. In any case, it is unlikely to
conceive the independence movement without the participation of the **commercial bourgeoisie** Creole of these cities. It
is not correct, therefore, to assert that independence was made
by the agro-exporting group.

Equally, the second statement of the paragraph is not correct either. The struggle between liberals and conservatives,
which is being pursued both in Colombia and in almost all
countries of Latin America, is nothing more than the political expression, as Sunkel maintains, of the struggle between
the **traditional oligarchy** and the **modern oligarchy**. At this
point we completely agree with this author.

---

(27) Fernando H. Cardoso, *Presentación de los comentarios y discusiones de
la cuarta y quinta sesiones [Presentation of the comments and discussions of
the fourth and fifth sessions]*, en **Las clases sociales en América Latina [In
Social classes in Latin America]. Problemas de conceptualización [Problems
of conceptualization]** (Seminario de [Seminary of] Mérida, Yucatán) Instituto
de Investigaciones Sociales, U.N.A.M. [Institute of Social Research, U.N.A.M.];
coordinado por [Coordinated by] Raúl Benítez Zenteno, Siglo [Century] XXI, la.
Ed. p. 426, México, 1973.

(28) Fernando H. Cardoso y Enzo Faletto, **Dependencia y Desarrollo en América Latina [Dependence and Development in Latin America]**, Siglo [Century]
XXI, 6a. ed., p. 75; México 1972.

"Liberals," says Sunkel, *"who are influenced by the ideas prevailing in Europe and the United States, and often alien to the reality of their own countries, are in part an intellectual group and partly represent the interests of* **agricultural and mining exporters , As well as those linked to foreign trade and finance, which are largely in English hands.** *Conservatives express interests that try to maintain a model that could be called "mercantilist-national," an extension of the colonial system after political independence.* **They rely on the bureaucracy itself formed during the colonial period; on the privileged traders during the same and the great traditional landlords and landowners, whose form of paternalistic organization within the hacienda appears as incompatible with the liberal conceptions of contract, of work, of equality before the law and of individual freedom"**.[29]

The interpretation errors of Cardoso and Faletto derive, in our opinion, from the imprecision of the concepts of traditional oligarchy and modern oligarchy, from the lack of understanding of the nature of these classes and the role they play in the process of independence of America Latina.

However, the triumph of liberalism in Latin America, particularly in Mexico, represents the political triumph of the modern oligarchy, that is, the social displacement of the landlord aristocracy that retained power during the first phase of republican life. This, however, did not imply social disruption or the elimination of large estate, that is, the transformation of the economic structure that served as the basis for the large

---

(29) Osvaldo Sunke y Pedro Paz, **El Subdesarrollo latinoamericano y la teoría del desarrollo** [Latin American Underdevelopment and Development Theory]; Siglo XXI Editores [21ˢᵗ Century Publishers], S.A., primera edición [first edition]; p. 302; México, 1970. (Negritas de JETA [JETA Bold])

landowners.[30] Aníbal Pinto is right when he states that "between these economic factions there are differences and frictions, but not deep contradictions"[...].[31]

"The traditional large estate," added Furtado, "of mainly subsistence economy, will always be marginal in the system of power that was formed in Brazil." However, since the new export agriculture is structured in large units, and the old large

-----

(30) El propósito explícito de las reformas liberales consistió en liberar la tierra de todas las trabas legales y consuetudinarias que impedían su dominio útil. Se iniciaron con el golpe de muerte a la institución económica más poderosa del viejo régimen: los intereses seculares de la iglesia. Las medidas contra la iglesia cumplían, además, un propósito político: debilitar el poder temporal más importante que obstaculizaba la consolidación del nuevo régimen. Del conjunto de disposiciones de la nueva constelación del poder, la más inmediata fue la supresión de los diezmos a favor de la iglesia, que gravaba tanto la producción agrícola como el valor de la propiedad privada; fue suprimida la alcabala territorial, los arrendamientos perpetuos, las vinculaciones y bienes de manos muertas y se decretó la total libertad de movimiento de las personas. El sistema de manos muertas residía en la posesión por parte de la iglesia y sus congregaciones monásticas de bienes y propiedades de católicos, que eran cedidos por herencia y que le pertenecían a aquella a perpetuidad. Una vez repartidos los latifundios religiosos en forma de renta o adjudicación gratuita se prosiguió a liberar la propiedad cedida en censo, es decir, la tierra entregada de manera perpetua mediante el pago de un cánon annual [The explicit purpose of the liberal reforms was to free the land from all legal and customary obstacles that impeded its useful mastery. They began with the death blow to the most powerful economic institution of the old regime: the secular interests of the church. Measures against the church also served a political purpose: to weaken the most important temporal power that hampered the consolidation of the new regime. Of the set of provisions of the new constellation of power, the most immediate was the suppression of the tithes in favor of the church, which taxed both agricultural production and the value of private property; The territorial alcabala, the perpetual leases, the bonds and goods of dead hands were suppressed and the total freedom of movement of the people was decreed. The system of dead hands resided in the possession by the church and its monastic congregations of goods and properties of Catholics, which were ceded by inheritance and belonged to that in perpetuity. Once the religious large estates were distributed in the form of a free rent or allotment, the property released by census was continued, that is to say, the land delivered in perpetuity through the payment of an annual fee].

(31) Aníbal Pinto, Ob. Cit. p. 38.

estates a fundamental solidarity, which allowed them to retain control of local power in the respective regions, corresponding to that hegemonic control of national power".[32]

However, it would not be correct to argue, as the author points out, that the fundamental solidarity established between the old large estates and the new export agriculture is due to the fact that the latter is "structured in large units", for the same solidarity is found when the export sector is linked to mining or between these elements and importers traders.

If a political and family merger takes place between the old and the new oligarchy, this is explained by the fact that the process that engenders the liberal oligarchy does not destroy the old feudal structure. The export sector emerges as an appendage of the central economies, that is to say, detached from the material spheres of domestic production. The capital invested in this sphere in the form of **productive capital** does not multiply or reproduce in the rest of the **productive sectors** of the economy; Escapes from the productive sphere to the sphere of circulation or to the circuit of unproductive expenditures. That is why capital investment in the export sector is not incompatible with pre-capitalist forms of exploitation; Conversely, it can assume any of the possible relations of combination: the same thing gives a modern capitalist enterprise as a slave plantation or semi-capitalist large estate in which capitalist and feudal forms of exploitation are mixed. Often the capitalist finds this latter type of large estates more advantageous, which guarantees him, as a consequence of the low assimilation of technology and, consequently, of the low organic composition of capital, a high rate of exploitation, that

---

(32) Celso Furtado, **La Economía Latinoamericana de la Conquista Ibérica hasta la Revolución Cubana [The Latin American Economy of the Iberian Conquest to the Cuban Revolution]**; Editorial Universitaria [University Publishing], la ed. en español [The Ed. In Spanish], p; 42; Santiago de Chile, 1969.

is, of profit. That is the economic basis for the social fusion of oligarchic groups of a different nature.

Some authors who recognize the anti-national character of the commercial bourgeoisie *([...] "the antinational role that this economic-political sector has played in the city of Buenos Aires, throughout our history"),*[33] attributed, however, a developed **feeling National of a defensive character** to the Buenosairean landowners.

*"Connected to the country because of their **interests and their psychology**," says Abelardo Ramos, "if, in the face of the poor provinces, they wanted to maintain port and customs privileges, they had instead a **developed national sense of defensive character**".*[34]

Moreover, **"nationalism rancher"** is the title of a chapter of his work.[35]

[...] "The Buenos Aires landlords [...]," the author maintains in credit to his point of view, "although they sold their products in foreign markets, in the first place, were direct producers of the only important branch of the Argentine economy of that time".[36]

The logic of this argumentation would lead one to think that the export bourgeoisies of the underdeveloped countries

---

(33) Jorge Ablardo Ramos, *Revolución y contrarrevolución en la Argentina [Revolution and counterrevolution in Argentina]; Tomo [Volume] 1:* **Historia de la Argentina en el siglo XIX [History of Argentina in the 19th century];** Editorial Plus Ultra; 3a. ed., p. 89; Buenos Aires, 1965.]

(34) Ibid., p. 89. Cursivas de JETA [JETA Italics].

(35) Ibid., p. 119. Ramos se refiere en este capítulo al debatido gobierno de Rosas [Ramos refers in this chapter to the debated government of Rosas].

(36) Ibid., p.89.

would be constituted in **national bourgeoisie** as direct producers of the most important branch of the economy. This position seems to me completely erroneous. **The modern oligarchy is by nature antinational**. It is not their investment in the productive sphere that determines their behavior, but their congenital bond with the world market, that is to say, their total detachment from the internal market. At this point we fully agree with Claudio Véliz.

This is how the Chilean oligarchy describes this author.

"During the years between the independence of 1829 the Chilean economy was dominated by three groups of fundamental importance: the three legs of the national economic table, first the mining exporters from the north of the country, then the agricultural exporters of the south, and finally the large importing firms, generally located in the center of Santiago and Valparaiso, although they operated throughout the territory. Mining exporters in the north of the country, according to Claudio Véliz, were free traders. This position was not due primarily to doctrinal reasons, although there were also, but also to the simple fact that these gentlemen were endowed with common sense: they exported copper, silver, saltpeter, and other minor minerals to Europe and the United States, where they received their payment in pounds sterling. Relying on reasons so solidly entrenched in common sense and further reinforced by liberal environmental doctrine, northern mining exporters continued to dress in London, decorating their wives in Paris, furnishing their houses in Italy, liking French wines and liqueurs at their tables, importing satins, velvets, costume jewelry and glassware, all generously paid for with the rich metallic viscera of our hard northern territory. The agricultural exporters in the south of the country were also decidedly free traders. They put their wheat and flour in Europe, California and Australia. They dressed their

cowboys with ponchos of English cloth; Mounted on chairs made by the best London saddlers; they consumed real champagne and illuminated their mansions with Florentine lamps. At night they slept in beds made by excellent English cabinetmakers, among sheets of Irish thread and wrapped in blankets of English wool. Their silk shirts came from Italy and the jewels and ornaments of their women from London, Paris and Rome. **For these landlords paid in pounds sterling the idea of taxing the export of wheat or imposing protectionist rights on imports was simply worthy of an asylum [...].. For these simple reasons of irreproachable solidity, the agricultural exporter of the South was fully in agreement with the mining exporter of the north and both pressured the government so that Chile maintained a free trade policy.** *The large import companies based in Valparaíso and Santiago were also free trade. Would one imagine an importing firm defending the establishment of strong import rights to protect a national industry".* [37]

"For this reason, among other things, the arrival and consolidation of foreign interests in our country did not have the painful characteristics that so dramatically illustrated the imperialist phenomenon during the nineteenth century [...] Here the foreign interventionists and the leaders of the Chilean economic tripod They spoke the same language: their interests coincided and there was no possible conflict. The one who was most concerned with granting facilities was the Chilean leader of some or all of the three fundamental pressure groups. The Chilean was the one who insisted that they should not be paid Import or export rights, the Chilean was the one who abhorred any attempt to protect

---

(37) Claudio Véliz, *La mesa de tres Patas [The three-legged table],* en la revista **Desarrollo Económico** [In the **Economic development** magazine], abril-septiembre [April-September], p. 237 y ss; Argentina, 1963. Cursivas de JETA [JETA Italics].

the incipient national industry, the Chilean was the one who was concerned primarily that the regular flow of raw materials to the European markets would not be interrupted".[38] There cannot be, therefore, no doubt about the anti-national and foreign character of the social classes that make up the modern oligarchy.

Some authors consider that the modern oligarchy is a group **without own power, subordinate and dependent** on the great financial and industrial centers of the capitalist metropolis.

"Real power," says Bresani, referring to the Peruvian oligarchy, "the decisive decision-making power escapes our analysis, because it always flees backwards, moving in the end to the outside, where it is lost again in another network of relations [...]. In short, what remains in our hands and which we consider as an 'oligarchy', is only a set of intermediaries (a mass without its own power) [...] and only able to negotiate the conditions sometimes almost imposed and sometimes almost begged, in That the imported decisions will be made [...].[39] *"In any case," adds Denis, referring to the Caribbean oligarchies, "the Creole oligarchies [...] are actually dependent oligarchies, contingent, though not for that, on the majority of the less allied cases of the oligarchies that dictate the conditions from the great financial and industrial centers of the capitalist metropolis".*[40]

---

(38) Claudio Véliz, Ob. Cit., pp. 240-241. Cursivas de JETA [JETA Italics].

(39) Jorge Braso Bresani, *Mito y realidad de la oligarquía peruana [Myth and reality of the Peruvian oligarchy]*; en [in] José Matos Mar, **La oligarquía en el Perú [The oligarchy in Peru]**; Editorial Diógenes, 2a. Ed., p. 86; México, 1970.

(40) Manuel Maldonado Denis, *Hacia un esbozo de las oligarquías en el Caribe Hispano parlante [Towards an outline of the oligarchies in the Spanish-speaking Caribbean]*, en **Revista Mexicana de Sociología** [in **Mexican Journal of Sociology**], Vol. [Volume] XXX, No. 1, p. 80; enero-mayo de [January-May] 1968.

In my opinion, this position is not sustainable. We have already said that the modern oligarchy, by its congenital nature, is linked to the great centers of the capitalist metropolises. For this reason it is **free trade, antinational, and foreign,** and for that reason, its interests, as Favre points out referring to the Peruvian oligarchy[...] **"far from being opposed to those of foreign companies, are unified and combine intimately, without necessarily being dependent or subordinate"**.[41] The case of the Gildemeister family company cited by Favre in this regard.

"The Gildemeister, whose fortune is linked to the exploitation of the saltpeter of Tarapacá, owns 32,213 acres, which are cultivated and are the first sugar producers in Peru. The vessels belonging to the Gildemeister, in part, transport it to Chile, where it is treated in The Gildemeister refinery and marketed by a Gildemeister company. With regard to the other part, it is sent to Germany, where the Gildemeister owns various shares in the chemical industry, on vessels flying the German flag but also belonging to the Gildemeister. In addition, these same ships ensure the transport to Hamburg of the sugar from the plantations that the Gildemeister own in Brazil. The Gildemeister Company can be advantageously compared, from any point of view, with the United Fruit Co. or with other large American corporations operating on an international scale".[42]

Thus, contrary to what some of its virtual opponents have been led to believe, the oligarchy is not a minority without its own power, subject to foreign monopolies, but a group of

---

(41) Henri Favre, *Misteriosa oligarquía [Mysterious oligarchy]*, en [in] José Matos Mar, Ob. Cit., p. 180. Cursivas de JETA [JETA Italics].

(42) Henri Favre, *El desarrollo y las formas del poder oligárquico en el Perú [The development and forms of oligarchic power in Peru]*, en [in] José Matos Mar, Ob. cit., p. 115.

social classes that has subordinated the interests of the nation to its Economic interests.

"But it is not the fact that the government has controlled what really distinguishes the men of coffee," says Furtado. ***"What sets them apart is that they have used that control to achieve clearly defined objectives in a policy; because of that class consciousness of their own interests, they differ from other dominant or former dominant groups".***[43]

We now have to summarize what we have said about the modern oligarchy.

From the preceding cases that we have analyzed, it is not difficult to perceive the following particular, general and essential characteristics.

1) The modern oligarchy emerges as a social expression of monoproduction, once implemented, after the Industrial Revolution, the new international division of labor that it imposes as a result of the process of integration of the world economy.

2) This oligarchy is formed from the export-import sector that is born linked to the world market. Hence its bourgeois-modern character that distinguishes it, in everything and everything, from the "traditional-feudal" oligarchy.

Any definition that one tries to give on the modern oligarchy must gather in its content these essential traits.

---

(43) Celso Furtado, **Formación Económica del Brasil [Economic Formation of Brazil]**; Fondo de Cultura Económica [Fund of Economic Culture]; 1ª.ed. en español [in Spanish], pp. 122-123; México, 1962.

To clarify this, we can say that **the modern oligarchy is no more than the social expression of monoproduction, formed by the export-importing antinational bourgeoisie that emerged after the Industrial Revolution, when the new international division of labor was introduced as a direct result of the process of integration of the world economy.**

It is evident, therefore, that the discovery of the specific and responsible social classes of underdevelopment in the **"period", "style" or "model of expansion or outward development",** that is, of the **modern oligarchy**, allows us not only to demystify ECLAC's theory of *'the concentration of technical progress and its fruits in export-oriented economic activities' as the main cause of underdevelopment* [44] and to

---

(44) "La cosmovisión de la economía internacional –subraya Celso Furtado-, en la que se afirmaba la existencia de una ruptura estructural causada por la lenta propagación del progreso técnico y que se veía perpetuada por la división internacional del trabajo, **fue el principal aporte teórico de Prebisch y constituyó el punto de partida de la teoría del subdesarrollo, que asumió una posición preponderante en el pensamiento de América Latina de la posguerra. Para Prebisch, el subdesarrollo se origina en 'la concentración del progreso técnico y sus frutos en actividades económicas orientadas hacia la exportación', dando lugar a estructuras sociales heterogéneas 'en virtud de las cuales una gran parte de la población es mantenida al margen del desarrollo'** ["The worldview of the international economy," says Celso Furtado, "which affirmed the existence of a structural rupture caused by the slow propagation of technical progress and perpetuated by the international division of labor, **was the main theoretical contribution of Prebisch and constituted the starting point of the theory of underdevelopment, which assumed a preponderant position in postwar Latin American thought. For Prebisch, underdevelopment stems from 'the concentration of technical progress and its fruits in export-oriented economic activities', giving rise to heterogeneous social structures, whereby a large part of the population is kept out of development'**]". (Celso Furtado, *La cosmovisión de Prebisch [Prebisch's worldview]*, en Banco Interamericano de Desarrollo [In Inter-American Development Bank], **El legado de [The legacy of] Raúl Prebisch**; Enrique V. Iglesias Editor; pp. 52-53; Washington, D.C., 1993.Negritas de JETA [JETA Bold]). **La lenta propagación del progreso técnico en la periferia como punto de partida y principal debilidad de la concepción del subdesarrollo de la CEPAL [The slow spread of tech-**

explain why the capitalist system did not follow in the peripheral economies the path of development foreseen by Marx; But to unravel our deepest secrets of our modern history: the Balkanization of Latin America, that is to say, the failure of the Bolivarian ideology and the intense class struggle that happens to it.

Here is its historical synthesis.

4. *THE FAILURE OF THE BOLIVARIAN IDEAL: THE VULCANIZATION OR FRAGMENTATION OF LATIN AMERICA.*

At the beginning of the independence movement, all the great leaders carried the national project in their heads. He deceives in Chile, Bolívar in Gran Colombia, Artigas, Monteagudo, San Martin and Dean Funes in the United Provinces, Morazán in Central America. The initiates, moreover, are children of the century who witness the process of culmination of nations in Europe. It is only natural that they embody this movement in Latin America. It is not surprising, then, that the day after the funeral of Colombia; Bolivar put into practice his intention to begin the Confederation of New Spanish-American States.

---

nical progress in the periphery as a starting point and main weakness of ECLAC's conception of underdevelopment], es el título del segundo trabajo de la serie *Contribución a la crítica de la concepción del subdesarrollo de la CEPAL* [Is the title of the second work of the series *Contribution to the critique of the conception of underdevelopment of ECLAC*], que hemos venido publicando [that we have been publishing].

"The Association of the Five States of America," he wrote to O'Higgins, "is so sublime in it-self that I am sure it will be a source of astonishment for Europe". [(45)]

Bolivar's dream was to found a Confederation of Five Great States on the basis of public law recognized in America, to respect the limits of the former viceroyalties, captaincies, or presidencies like that of Chile.

The idea took shape in the Amphicryonic Congress of Panama, which unanimously approved the *Treaty of Union, League, and Perpetual Confederation on July 15, 1826 between the Republics of Peru, Colombia, Central America, and the United Mexican States*, who's Article, read as follows:

---

(45) Bolivar, **Documentos [Documents]**, p. 107, Ed. Casa de las Américas [House of the Americas]; La Habana [Havana]. Esta idea ya era suya desde mucho antes. En **1815**, en su carta de Jamaica, **Contestación de un americano meridional a un caballero de esta Isla**, apuntaba [This idea was already his long before. In **1815**, in his letter from Jamaica, **Reply of a South American to a knight of this Island**, stated]: "es una idea grandiosa pretender formar de todo el Mundo Nuevo una sola nación con un solo vínculo que ligue sus partes entre sí y con el todo. Ya que tiene un origen, una lengua, unas costumbres y una religión, debería, por consiguiente, tener un solo gobierno que confederase los diferentes estados que hayan de formarse; más no es posible, porque climas remotos, situaciones diversas, intereses opuestos, caracteres desemejantes dividen a la América. ¡Qué bello sería que el Istmo de Panamá fuese para nosotros lo que el de Corinto para los griegos! ¡Ojalá que algún día tengamos la fortuna de instalar allí un augusto congreso de los representantes de las repúblicas, reinos e imperios a tratar y discutir sobre los altos intereses de la paz y la guerra! ["It is a grand idea to try to form a single nation of the whole New World with a single bond that connects its parts to each other and to the whole, since it has an origin, language, customs and religion, To have a single government that would confederate the different states to be formed, but it is not possible, because remote climates, diverse situations, opposing interests, unlike characters divide the Americas. How beautiful would it be that the Isthmus of Panama was for us what The Corinthians for the Greeks! May we one day be fortunate enough to set up there an august congress of representatives of the republics, kingdoms and empires to treat and discuss the high interests of peace and war!]" (Ibid., p. 61).

"The Republics of Peru, Colombia, Central America and the United Mexican States, bind themselves and confederate each other in peace and war, and contract for this a perpetual pact of firm and unchanging friendship and of close and intimate union in each and every one of the parties".[46]

This was the first and only firm step in the crystallization of the great idea of the American Confederation. The decadence and dissipation of that sublime ideal has been fatal and progressive.

"Miranda had been the apostle of the brotherhood; Monteagudo was his tribune, Bolivar his Caesar as Flores was after his Judas and Walker his bloody storyteller".[47]

The treaty of perpetual Union, League, and Confederation approved by the Congress of Panama was to be ratified and ratifications exchanged in the Villa of Tacubaya, a league away from Mexico City, within the term of eight months counted from the date of its signature or earlier if possible.

---

(46) **Colección de Ensayos y Documentos Relativos a la Unión y Confederación de los Pueblos Hispanoamericanos [Collection of Essays and Documents Relating to the Union and Confederation of Spanish-American Peoples]** , publicada a expensas de la [Published at the expense of] *Sociedad de la Unión Americana de Santiago de Chile [Society of the American Union of Santiago de Chile]*, por la Comisión nombrada por la misma y compuesta de los señores Don José Victorino Lastarria, Don Alvaro Covarrubias, Don Domingo Santa María y Don Benjamín Vicuña Mackenna ta [By the Commission appointed by the same and composed of Don Jose Victorino Lastarria, Don Alvaro Covarrubias, Don Domingo Santa Maria and Don Benjamín Vicuña Mackenna ta]; Santiago de Chile, 1862. Esta es una edición de la revista [This is an issue of the magazine] **Tareas [Chores]** en Conmemoración al Sesquicentenario del Congreso Anfictiónico de Panamá [In Commemoration of the Sesquicentennial of the Amphictyonic Congress of Panama], p. 38; Panamá, 1976.

(47) Benjamín Vicuña Mackenna, *Estudios Históricos [Historical Studies]*, en **Colección de Ensayos y Documentos Relativos a la Unión y Confederación de los Pueblos Hispanoamericanos [In Collection of Essays and Documents Relating to the Union and Confederation of the Spanish-American Peoples]**, p. 148.

"Quotations had been made to continue and top up their arduous enterprise in the picturesque village of Tacubaya, which is close to the capital of Mexico, but the discord which later devastated this country (and the rest of the Continent - JETA) Magnificent and ill-fated purposes". [48]

Benign climates for Latin American unity had long since disappeared. All the forces that Bolivar managed to assemble around him to consummate the independence, dissolved when he tried to construct the unit of the newly emancipated States. The same regional oligarchies that supported the liberating armies with resources and men, including many parish "fathers of the fatherland", turned against the unifiers when free trade was guaranteed. The dissociating centers of Latin American unity are basically Buenos Aires, Caracas, Bogotá and Lima. The chain of export ports of raw materials and importers of English manufactures -Valparaiso, Arica, Callao, Guayaquil, Cartagena, Puerto Cabello, La Guaira, Bahia, Santos, Montevideo, Buenos Aires- tended irresistibly to the world market and to necessarily establish tariffs Political regime consistent with this trend. Political centralization could only be the result of an economy converging with the internal market, that is to say, founded on an industrial capitalist production; hence, the historical responsibility of the modern oligarchy in the process of Balkanization of Hispanic America.

However, a question arises that regional thinking must answer: **why was Latin America fragmented and Portuguese America did not?**

Here is the answer from Celso Furtado.

The Spanish colonial enterprise was based on the exploitation of the labor force of the occupied territories. Spain did not

---

(48) Ibid., p. 151.

become interested in promoting an exchange with or between the colonies, and the forms in which the relationships between the Metropolis and the colonies were organized created a permanent shortage of means of transport and were the cause of excessively high freight rates. Spanish policy was oriented to transform the colonies into self-sufficient economic systems and producers of a net surplus in the form of precious metals that was periodically transferred to the Metropolis. That is why the economic decline of Spain harmed its American colonies. Outside of the mining operation, no other major economic enterprise came to be realized. During the three centuries of life of the great colonial empire, agricultural exports throughout the immense region at no time reached significant importance. The supply of manufactures from the large masses of the indigenous population continued to be based on local handicrafts, which delayed the transformation of the preexisting subsistence economies in the region.[49]

Gold and silver production, as the trade and export of minerals from America to Spain, began to decline around the middle of the seventeenth century. Mexico will still know a brilliant phase in the last century of the colonial era as an exporter of silver, but for Upper Peru the great era had ended. The decline of mining production meant the collapse of the economic system that emerged in the vast region. Weakened demand for agricultural and Indian surpluses for mining and transportation, *entrustment* as an institution tended to lose its importance. In fact, the *entrustment* system was conceived in the idea that part of the surplus from the Indians belonged to the Crown, which transfigured the grant holder into a collecting agent. Atrophied the markets that previously allowed to monetize the surplus, the transfer of a part of the same to the

---

(49) Celso Furtado, **Formación Económica del Brasil [Economic Formation of Brazil]**, Fondo de Cultura Económica [Fund of Economic Culture], 2a. Ed., en español [in Spanish], pp. 21 -22; México, 1974.

State was transformed into an annoying load. The Institution then tended to decay to formally disappear at the beginning of the eighteenth century. The decadence of the economic system organized around the "poles" producing precious metals took the form of a progressive decentralization of the economic and social activities that turned land ownership into the basic institution of the entire social order. The control of land ownership made it possible to continue the extraction of surplus of the indigenous population once the *entrustment* regime had been eliminated. As the surplus, by its very nature, was to be used locally almost in its entirety, the social structure tended to take the form of isolated or semi-isolated units. These large rural areas of essentially rural economy, almost totally unrelated to state authority, must be deeply rooted in Latin American society.[50]

In Portuguese America the evolution of this process followed an inverse line. The large slave plantation turned to the outside declined in the second half of the XVII century, as a result of the bankruptcy of the sugar monopoly and the fall in the prices of that product. The production of the French and English West Indies grows rapidly from that time, while the mercantilist policy closes much of the European markets to the sugar from the Portuguese colony. The loss of foreign markets resulted in the disintegration of part of the export agriculture and its transformation into a natural economy. The sector that produced meat, traction animals and fuelwood for the coastal units suffered involution even faster. The discovery of gold at the beginning of the eighteenth century favorably modified the trend of this general evolution. An important market for traction animals was created and conditions emerged to occu-

---

(50) Celso Furtado, **La Economía Latinoamericana desde la Conquista Ibérica hasta la Revolución Cubana [The Latin American Economy from the Iberian Conquest to the Cuban Revolution]**; Ed. Universitaria [University Edition]; p. 30; Santiago, Chile, 1969.

py the underemployed labor force of the sugar economy. The San Francisco River that links the cattle region of the northeast to the mining area became an important communication route. Unlike the production of sugar that was only accessible to those who could mobilize large financial resources, alluvial gold could be exploited at both the artisanal and large-scale levels. Portuguese emigration to the region took place on a much larger scale than in the previous two centuries. Urban life was developed and a food market was formed that joined the traction market for the extensive transport system linking the vast gold region with the port of Rio de Janeiro. This animal market was mainly supplied by the southern regions whose possibilities for livestock production were already known. In this way, the mining pole allowed the formation of economic links between the northeast, central and southern Brazilian territory as early as the 18th century.[51]

On the other hand, the policy of the Brazilian Empire tried to reconcile the interests of the different local aristocracies (the sugar of the north, the cattle of the center and the cattle of the south end). Among these adversaries who also collided with the small and medium-sized trade in the ports, a certain balance was possible which the Crown maintained with the support of the army, little nationalized and mixed, not coincidentally, with European mercenary corps. Resistance to the suppression of the slave trade had facilitated the maintenance of that balance in the agitated decades of 1830 and 1840. Slavery was essential to the sugar economy of the north and the center coast; The beginning of the expansion of coffee (which was insinuated in Rio de Janeiro before finding its land of choice in Sao Paulo) also relied on slave labor. At the same time, the slave trade, which British persecution was both more risky and more profitable, offered a timely revenge to Portuguese merchants of the coastal cities, which were eliminated

---

(51) Ibid., p. 32.

from the great European commerce by the British. When this community of interests began to crack by the end of the 1840s, the conditions for territorial fragmentation no longer existed.

The increasing persecution of the slave trade, at the same time put in crisis the agriculture that used that labor more and more expensive. This growing divergence of fates and interests brought an end to the gentle rebellion of the parliamentarians who -conservatives or liberals- agreed to call for effective measures against trafficking; These finally arrived in 1851. Slave farming was becoming unsustainable.[52]

The very evolution of the social production system was thus creating in the case of the Spanish Empire the material premises of its Balkanization, while in the case of the Portuguese Empire, conditions that favored the preservation of its territorial unit. In the latter case, it should be added that when the coffee oligarchy consolidated in the third quarter of the last century, the Brazilian government was subject to overly heterogeneous interests and the conditions for the fragmentation of its territory no longer existed.

The power of British penetration in South America, at the outbreak of the nineteenth century, was as irresistible as the maritime and industrial force on which it was based. Where the Creoles took power and controlled the territory, the doors to the English trade and to the consul of the Empire were opened. There were two reasons at the beginning for this policy: first, the fiscal needs of the new States which the free trade of the Spanish barriers met with certain abundance. The second was that Great Britain, by virtue of its commercial interests, appeared as the main obstacle to the conclusion of a Holy

---

(52) Tulio Halperin Donghi, **Historia Contemporánea de América Latina [Contemporary History of Latin America]**; Ed. Alianza [Alliance Edition]; 4a. Ed,, pp. 166-167; Madrid, 1975.

Alliance of reactionary Europe against the Spanish colonies. The great European power was formally indifferent to the fate of the newly liberated Spanish colonies; But unofficially sold arms and obtained markets for their manufactures. The question of Latin American markets was increasingly being imposed on the conditions of the Foreign Office. If in 1805 the value of English exports to Latin America amounted to 7,771,418 pounds sterling, in 1810 they reached 34,061,901 sterling pounds. It was considered in London that this fabulous contingent of Spanish speech could absorb more English goods than India and the United States It was impossible for England to ignore that continent, especially after the continental blockade decreed by Napoleon and the elevation by the United States of a harsh protectionist barrier against its former metropolis. These circumstances explain the role that Britain played throughout the nineteenth century in the life of Latin America.

"Hispanic-America," says Hobsbawm, "came to depend almost entirely on British imports during the Napoleonic wars, and after its rupture with Spain and Portugal became an almost total economic dependence on England, isolated from any political interference of potential competitors of the latter country. In 1820 the 'impoverished continent' already acquired more than a quarter of British cotton cloth than Europe, in 1840 it would acquire half of Europe [...] The expansion of English industry could easily be financed in the margin of the current profits, by the combination of the conquests of their vast markets and a continuous inflation of prices producing fantastic profits. It was not only or ten percent, but hundreds and millions of percent who made Lancashire his fortunes".[53]

---

(53) Eric J. Hobsbawm, **Las Revoluciones Burguesas [The Bourgeois Revolutions],** Editorial Guadarrama [Editorial Guadarrama], p. 57; Madrid, 1964.

The classic Balkanizing policy of the British Empire, already practiced in the Iberian Peninsula, found in the weakened American colonies an optimal occasion. The English only moved subtly in the great drama and maintained the policy of the dissociating oligarchies, when they did not suggest the formula, as happened with the tearing of the Eastern Band.

[...] "It is convenient to observe," points out Furtado, "that English penetration in the first decades of the nineteenth century constituted much more an element of disaggregation of the existing social and economic order [...] The English presence was manifested essentially in the organization of a trade Importer houses appeared that spread the manufactures in clothes, mainly English, changing habits of consumption and causing the disintegration of local artisan activities. In many countries, the pressure of increased imports led to exchange depreciation and forced governments to borrow from abroad to regularize the balance of payments situation. On the other hand, the importing houses of English products accumulated liquid reserves and were transformed into powerful financial centers".[54]

These are the propitious historical conditions in which the modern oligarchy operate, of the port cities of the continent.

"The peculiarities of the port," says Abelardo Ramos, "its customs and renting power, its indifference to the provinces and Latin America, its status as producer, exporter and importer will turn the interests of Buenos Aires into one of the driving factors of the Balkanization. From the Buenos Aires will, the Uruguayan 'Nation', the Bolivian 'Nation', and the Paraguayan 'Nation' will be born. Buenos Aires harasses the call of the Congress of Panama and the effort of San Martin to liberate Peru, manages a European prince to crown

---

(54) Celso Furtado, Ob. cit., p. 39.

in The Plata, fights Artigas allied with the Portuguese and concludes by exterminating Paraguay in 1865 with the same allies [...] The 'Mantuan' class betrays Bolivar and undoes Gran Colombia, the stakeholders of the Eastern Band take a stab at atheism, the men for pro sweep away Carrera, and assassinate Manuel Rodríguez in Chile, Artigas sinks into the Paraguayan jungle, Paraguay is placed defensively under the iron fist of Dr. Francia, San Martín emigrates, Morazán is assassinated and the Republic of Central America explodes in five pieces, Mexico is isolated and agonized a century under the landowners [...] .. The foreign powers, United States and Great Britain, dispute the territory and economy of the twenty republics that Bolivar had dreamed of being united. After its independence, balkanization ensues. Latin America becomes an unfinished nation". [55]

The viceroyalty of New Granada, which included the audience of Santa Fe de Bogota, the provinces of Panama and San Francisco de Quito, and the Command of Caracas, was definitively established in 1739 with its capital in Santa Fe de Bogota. Near the battle of Boyacá in the Congress of Angostura of 1819, Bolivar proposes to reunite the liberated provinces of New Granada to the provinces of Venezuela. "The meeting of New Granada and Venezuela is the only object that I have proposed since my first: it is the vote of the citizens of both countries and it is the guarantee of the freedom of South America." The former deputy to the Napoleonic courts of Bayonne, Francisco Antonio de Zea, and precursor of independence, responded ecstatically in the name of Congress: "If Quito, Santa Fe and Venezuela meet in a single republic, who

---

(55) Jorge Abelardo Ramos, **Historia de la Nación Latinoamericana [History of the Latin America Nation],** Ed. APL [APL Edition], p. 146; Argentina, 1968. Este libro es, sin lugar a duda, una de las obras más sugestivas sobre la historia de la balcanización de América Latina [This book is undoubtedly one of the most suggestive works on the history of the Balkanization of Latin America]

can calculate the power and Prosperity corresponding to such immense mass?".[56]

In this way, Bolivar renames the old Kingdom and Captaincy with the name of Colombia.

The great victory of Sucre resounded throughout the Continent with an unmatched echo. The story of 300 years of Spanish power ended in Ayacucho. What seemed impossible was already a reality. The excitement that aroused the victory of Ayacucho runs in the chronicles. When Bolivar received the news, he suffered an attack of true alienation: he tore off his military jacket, swore to his officers, ignorant of what had happened, that he would never wear his military uniform again, he started to dance alone, as if he were truly possessed.

Bolivar's shadow loomed. In government newspapers, the Liberator began to criticize more and more sharply. He was credited with "imperialist" views. At the same time it is noticed that the government of Rivadavia had nothing to act against Marshal Olañeta that guarded after Ayacucho its dominion over the provinces Alto Peruvian. On a symbolic basis, he provided money and resources for 600 men of infantry and cavalry, who with the Saltenan militias commanded by General Arenales guarded the border of northern Argentina.[57]

The Buenos Aires strategy sought to guarantee that border and that Sucre and Bolivar would end their independence at their cost. But the Congress meeting in Buenos Aires counted

---

(56) **Bolívar y la Emancipación de Sur-América [Bolivar and the Emancipation of South America]**, Memorias del Gral. O'Leary [Memories of General O'Leary, traducidas del inglés por su hijo Simón O'Leary [Translated from English by his son Simon O'Leary] (1819- 1826), p. 22, Tomo II y último [Volume II and last]; Madrid, Sociedad española de Librería [Spanish Society of Bookshop]; citado por [quoted by] Jorge Abelardo Ramos, Ob. cit., p. 169.

(57) Jorge Abelardo Ramos, Ob. Cit., pp. 221-222.

on some deputies who were not porteños. Deputy Castro affirmed: "I did not only propose that we put ourselves on the defensive, I proposed something else. I proposed as a necessity of the moment, not only the defense of our free territory, but the restitution of our occupied territory [...] In all the cases in which these provinces, now occupied by the enemy, have been pronounced have been pronounced as an integral part of our territory, so that in this assumption our congresses and assemblies have appointed alternates for them, and in its name has also been declared the independence of the country".[58] Such was the national position, which Bolivar would also support, but which rejected the Rivadaviana majority of the National Congress and the Executive Power itself.

For, in effect, Olañeta died by his own supporters, Sucre occupies with his forces, after Ayacucho, all the territory of the Upper Peru. In these circumstances, General Arenales wrote to the Argentine Government asking for orders, as "seditious men" promoted in Upper Peru their separation from the United Provinces. Sucre, meanwhile, writes to Bolivar:

"It seems that the province of Buenos Aires has calculated that it is not in their interests to gather these provinces to the Republic".[59]

"The Buenosairean bourgeoisie," says Abelardo Ramos, *"lacked any territorial concept of the Nation, since all its interests were projected towards Europe [...] Its invariable tendency was to reduce as much as possible the territorial area, to preserve the port and the Customs in Their hands, which provided most of the fiscal resources and rid the Mediterranean provinces, which lacked exportable products, to their*

---

(58) Gabriel René Moreno, **Ayacucho en [in] Buenos Aires**, p. 44, Ed. América [American Edition]; Madrid.

(59) Ibid., p. 127.

fate. Alto Peru thus became an irritating burden for the Bue-
nosairean". [60]

The Viceroyalty of the Rio de la Plata was divided in eight Intendancies, according to the French model adopted by the Spanish Bourbons. Outside the Intendance of Buenos Aires (including the Eastern Band) were included in the vice regal jurisdiction the following Intendancies: Intendancies of Paraguay (including thirteen of the 30 towns of the Missions); La Plata, or Charcas, then Chuquisaca the present Sucre; that of Cochabamba, including Santa Cruz de la Sierra; that of La Paz; the one of Potosí, with the rest of the High Peruvian territory. They were also the Intendances of Córdoba and Salta. The first included the territories of San Miguel de Tucumán, Jujuy, Santiago de Estero and Catamarca. The Intendance of Cordova included La Rioja, Mendozza, San Luis and San Juan. There were territories, such as Mojos and Chiquitos, which were under the direct command of the Viceroy, such as Montevideo and the Missions, in the form of military governorates, because they were border territories in dangerous relations with the Portuguese that dated back centuries of Iberian rivalries. The importance of Buenos Aires, as capital of the Viceroyalty, grew with the administrative dispositions of the Bourbons, who were judged the best equipped to serve as a political, military and revenue head of the viceroyalty: fertile field, city, port and unique customs. In fact, Buenos Aires was the only maritime city, so to speak, of a vast territory bottled between Lima and the Rio de la Plata. Of all the revolutionary committee established at the outbreak of the independence movement, the one in Buenos Aires was one of the few that had sufficient resources to face the expenses of the war immediately.

---

(60) Jorge Abelardo Ramos, Ob. cit., p. 227 y 223.

Well, before the pressures that were overwhelming him and in which he believed to see the opinion of the towns, Sucre decided to summon a Congress to the provinces Alto Peruvian, to *"decide of its fate"* and to *"sanction a regime of provisional government"*.[61]

The Minister of War of Bolivar, General Tomás Heres, wrote to Sucre by order of the Liberator, censoring the idea that *"it was the people of the four provinces of the Rio de la Plata, to which the liberty of establishing themselves should be left, because this would have been to make a terrible attack on the rights of the Argentine nation and to violate that of peoples, recognized until today in the America before the Spanish. V.S., giving the decree that he speaks to assemble an Assembly of the provinces of Upper Peru, commits an act of formal recognition of his sovereignty. [...] If this Assembly were to be held, the people would all be given a fateful example, which would weaken the association and foment anarchy [...] SE (Bolivar) sends me say that the matter of the four provinces of Upper Peru must remain in status quo, without making any innovation that directly or indirectly could prejudice the rights of the United Provinces of Rio de la Plata"*.[62]

But the clear exposition of Bolivarian policy against the Alto Peruvian provinces will be formulated by the Liberator in a letter dated February 2, 1825 to Sucre: *"Neither you nor I, nor the Congress of Peru, nor of Colombia, can break or violate the basis of the public right that we have recognized in America. This base is that the republican governments are founded between the limits of the old viceroyalties, captaincies general, or presidencies as the one of Chile. Upper Peru is a dependency of the Viceroyalty of Buenos Aires: immediate*

---

(61) Sabino Pinilla, **La creación de Bolivia [The creation of Bolivia],** Ed. América [American Edition], p. 102; Madrid.

(62) Ibid., p. 125.

dependence as that of Quito of Santa Fe. Chile, although it was dependent of Peru, already was separated of him some years before the revolution like Guatemala of the New Spain. Thus both or two of these presidencies have been able to be independent of their former viceroyalties, but neither Quito nor Charcas can be in justice, unless by agreement between parties, as a result of a war or a congress, a treaty can be entered into or concluded. As you say, you plan to convene an assembly in those provinces. Of course, the convocation itself is an act of sovereignty. In addition, calling these provinces to exercise their sovereignty, it separates them in fact from the other provinces of the Rio de la Plata. Of course, you will achieve with that measured bliss the disapproval of the Rio de la Plata, Peru, and Colombia itself, which you cannot even see with indifference, that you break the rights we have to the presidency of Quito by the old limits of the old viceroyalty".[63]

But Bolivar was wrong. No one, not even the Liberator, could conceive, despite how well Bolivar knew the political and social character of the Buenos Aires oligarchy, that it spontaneously renounced the reinstatement of Upper Peru to Argentine sovereignty. But it did. On May 9, 1825, the Rivas-Venezuelan Congress declared that *"although the four provinces of Upper Peru have always belonged to Argentina, it is the will of the General Constituent Congress that they remain in full freedom to dispose of their fate, to their interests and their happiness".[64] "Bolivar looked at the news of this law as a hoax that had been forged in Cordoba or Salta." He could not believe it! Sucre had to send the documents in authentic copies, and he surrendered to the evidence".[65]* Not yet recovered from his surprise, celebrating the arrival of the

---

(63) O'Leary, Ob. Cit., p. 439.

(64) Sabino Pinilla, Ob. cit., p. 139.

(65) Gabriel René Moreno, Ob. cit., p. 17.

Argentine mission led by Alvear in Potosi, the Liberator offered for *"the Congress of the United Provinces of the Rio de la Plata, whose liberality of principles is superior to all praise and whose detachment with respect to the provinces of Upper Peru is unheard of".* [(66)]

Summoned by Sucre, the Assembly of Deputies of Upper Peru delayed its meeting for a week, waiting for the news that awaited from Buenos Aires. On July 17, it was officially known that the port was disregarded of the fate of the provinces of Alto Peru. Drunk with joy, the separatist deputies set out to create a new state. In spite of Sucre's sympathies for another solution, the Assembly harbored the fear that Bolivar would resist approving the project; then began the deification of Bolivar. The new state fell on its knees before the Liberator, "the common father of Peru," "savior of the peoples," "firstborn son of the New World," "immortal Bolivar". The Assembly was presided over by Dr. José Ma. Serrano, former deputy for Charcas to the Congress of Tucumán, who in 1816 had declared the independence of the Provinces of South America, now turned into a furious separatist. Before Bolivar received flattery, the Assembly discussed the question of creating a new state. Most of the deputies who supported the independence of Upper Peru, followed by a minority that supported the incorporation of Peru and a smaller one, which supported the reinstatement of the United Provinces of Rio de la Plata. The Assembly finally decided to found the Bolivar Republic, thus offering its greatest tribute to the Liberator, who concluded by accepting the decision of the Assembly.[(67)] The province of Tarija, because of Bolivar's demands, was not included in the separatist maneuver. But it was lost the

---

(66) José Luis Busaniche, **Historia Argentina [Argentinian History]**, Ed. Hachette [Hachette Edition], p. 209.

(67) Jorge Abelardo Ramos, Ob. Cit., pp. 232-235.

following year of Argentine sovereignty, almost at the same time as the Eastern Band.

It is important to add that in that drama the English interference was very important. The British government was always so opposed to the legitimate demand of the Orientals to join the old United Provinces as to the inordinate ambition of the Empire of Brazil to extend its dominion to the Eastern Band. Its perennial ambition was to create a Gibraltar in the Eastern Band, an independent State that served as a wedge between Brazil and Argentina and that allowed Britain to weaken both and to have the best port of Rio de la Plata for its commerce. In a letter addressed by Canning to Ponsonby (the two architects of the project), he defined English policy in the following terms: *"The city and territory of Montevideo should definitely be independent of each country, in a situation somewhat similar to that of the Hanseatic cities in Europe".* [68]

Later, Canning himself repeated to Ponsonby:

"As V.E. knows, it has been suggested that Montevideo itself, or the entire Eastern Band, with Montevideo by Capital, be erected in a separate and independent state". [69]

By capturing his victorious military campaign and reaching the greatest political power of his hazardous career, Bolivar realized that his great unifying program had also come to an end. The attempt to impose on Peru, Gran Colombia and

---

(68) CK. Webster, **Gran Bretaña y la Independencia de América Latina [Great Britain and the Independence of Latin America]**, Documentos escogidos de los Archivos del Foreign Office [Documents selected from the Foreign Office Archives] (1812-1830); Tomo I [Volume I], Ed. Kraft [Kraft Edition], p. 196; Buenos Aires1944.

(69) Ibid.

Bolivia the Centralist Constitution that had conceived for the latter quickly triggered the disintegration of the whole system.

"The only remedy," he wrote, "is a General Federation between Bolivia, Peru, and Colombia, which is narrower than that of the United States, commanded by a president and vice-president and governed by the Bolivian Constitution that could serve the particular states and For the Federation". [70]

But in Peru, and particularly in Colombia, it was openly resisting the application of the Bolivian Constitution. The leader Llanero Paez intrigued in Caracas and the vice-president Santander did it in Bogota. The year 1826, when the Congress of Panama meets, is the year of the destruction of Gran Colombia. In Peru, the Peruvian military leaders who had emerged in the shadow of the Liberator conspired against him to break the ties that united Peru with Colombia and Bolivia. Like Venezuelan localism, Santander came from real separatism from raw material economies that could only be expanded to satisfy the needs of a rising world market. Santander was strong in the Senate and commerce, the two classic pillars of the Latin American oligarchies. The resistance of the Santander Liberal Party to the Bolivian Constitution manifests itself publicly with the cold reception organized on the arrival of Bolivar to Bogota; Bolivar's indignation at the intrigues of Santander made the Vice President fear the violent reaction of the Liberator upon his arrival at the Presidential Palace. [71] Bolivar had to leave immediately to Caracas to persuade General Paez to submit to his leadership. Under these circumstances, Colombian troops addicted to Santander revolt in Lima, overthrow the Bolivian Constitution and imprison General Heres, loyal to Bolivar. The Colombian-Peruvian-Bolivian federa-

---

(70) José Luis Busaniche, **Bolívar**, p. 226; citado por [quoted by] Jorge Abelardo Ramos, Ob. cit., p. 307.

(71) Jorge Abelardo Ramos, Ob. cit., pp. 307-308.

tion threatened to crumble. When Bolivar returned to Bogota, news arrived that in Lima a former subordinate of him, General La Mar was designated President of Peru, only to declare the Bolivian Constitution abolished. In January of 1827 the Cabildo of Quito organized a military conspiracy headed by Commander Ayarza with separatist purposes. The rest of the garrison repressed it by shooting those involved.

At that very moment Santander's supporters in Bogota were preparing to assassinate Bolivar in the Government Palace.[72] Bolivar was able to save his life thanks to the fortitude of his admirable companion Manuelita Saenz.

The Great Colombia crumbles to pieces. General Flores, a fervent Bolivarian, made the southern departments of Greater Colombia independent and founded the Republic of Ecuador. General Páez, surrounded by a nucleus that included the future president Antonio Leocadio Guzman, broke Venezuela's link with Colombia and refused any subordination to the Liberator. The separation of Venezuela was not by any means a popular decision. In order to carry it out, General Paez and his associates had carefully prepared the elections of the so-

---

(72) "Santander[...]..por sus manejos contra Bolívar había tenido que abandonar el país en 1826. Volvió como jefe de los liberales, con un programa de libertad y progreso[...]..Más que un soldado, Santander era un abogado. Era uno de tantos juristas que durante las guerras de liberación había tomado el oficio de las armas sin entender de él mucho en realidad. Pero aquel leguleyo era más desalmado y cruel que el soldado más rudo [Santander [...] for his maneuvers against Bolivar had to leave the country in 1826. He returned as head of the liberals, with a program of freedom and progress [...] More than a soldier, Santander was a lawyer. He was one of many jurists who during the liberation wars had taken the office of arms without much understanding of him. But that leglio was more soulless and cruel than the toughest soldier]" (Ernest Samhaber, **Sudamérica [South America], biografía de un continente [Biography of a continent]**, Ed. Sudamericana [South American Edition], p.472; Buenos Aires, 1961).

called "Constituent Congress of Venezuela," as that farce was called.[73]

Bolivar was physically and morally destroyed. But the Great Colombia was also annihilated. There were still a few strokes to his heart. That young General Cordova, who, at the pace of winners, decided with the lancers the battle of Ayacucho, and who had finished crushing Obando's sedition in Popayan, this same Cordoba rises in the province of Antioch against his former chief. There Córdoba died and with the young and legendary soldier the youth of Bolivar also died. In those days the Congress of Colombia rejects the resignation of Bolivar, but the Liberator no longer has the forces to take charge of the government and leaves the power in the hands of General Caicedo. Bolivar sought health away from Bogota. He had said farewell to Sucre that he was going to meet his wife in Quito. The Bogotá press, like Caracas, routinely insulted the Liberator and Sucre. These two fair names were enough to satisfy the scoundrel of the time and also for the judgment of history.

When crossing the province of Pasto without an escort, in which General Obando was governor, supporter of Santander, the Marshal of Ayacucho was shot to death by three subjects, the commander Morillo, the commander Juan Gregorio Sarria and Jose Brazo, man of the General Obando who had sent instructions in a closed document. General Obando was quick to deny all responsibility, since public opinion immediately blamed him for the horrendous crime. The officers of Obando's General Staff in Pasto were persuaded that he had been the instigator of the assassination; He abandoned the service

---

(73) Jorge Abelardo Ramos, Ob. Cit., pp. 313-314.

of New Granada en masse and moved to Ecuador. Morillo confessed his crime and was executed in 1842.[74]

Bolivar was near Cartagena when he received the news of the assassination of Sucre that annihilated him and precipitated his death. He was about to travel to Europe, although he was already lacking in resources, for he had given away his fifth, pawned his silverware, and distributed his last money among the multitude of officers, soldiers, and supporters fleeing the hostile Bogota. That "Mantuano" (White Creole) who at the beginning of the revolution had a thousand slaves, had released them all. Now, the slave-owners he refused to expropriate took him away from home. He only waited for a ship to get away from the land of his exploits. Feeling he's illness had worsen, he reached Santa Marta. There the doctors verified that his days were about to end. He died on December 17, 1830 in Santa Marta, in another's bed, free doctor, without a penny and with Gran Colombia divided into five States.

The decade after Bolivar's death will witness the founding and dissolution of the Peru-Bolivian Confederation and the fall of the Federal Republic of Central America.[75] Andrés de San-

---

(74) Antonio José de Irisarri, **Historia Crítica del Asesinato del Gran Mariscal de Ayacucho [Critical History of the Assassination of the Great Marshal of Ayacucho],** Ed. Casa de las Américas [House of the Americas Edition], p. 155; La Habana [Havana], 1964.

(75) La República Federal de Centroamérica era parte del virreinato de Nueva España establecido en 1535. Su territorio abarcó una gran extensión cuyo centro natural sería el valle de México. Sobre los cimientos de la monumental **Tenochtitlan** se erigió la ciudad de México, sede de la corte virreinal durante todo el período colonial. Los límites del virreinato comprendieron, por el sur, toda la América Central (Guatemala, El Salvador, Nicaragua, Honduras y Costa Rica), salvo la gobernación de Castilla de Oro con la estratégica ciudad de Panamá. Por el este, incluyó al golfo de México y al mar de las Antillas. Sin embargo, el territorio isleño compuesto por las pequeñas y grandes Antillas (Cuba, Santo Domingo y Puerto Rico entre otras), no formó parte de Nueva España, constituyendo gobernaciones independientes. Al norte, la jurisdicción de Nueva España

ta Cruz and Francisco de Morazán will be the central figures of both dramas. With the fall of Gran Colombia, independent Peru is torn by furious civil wars. The dissolution of Bolivar's unifying program seems to be unable to be stopped even within the petty frontiers achieved. Vice regal Peru is threatened by ceaseless military assaults and opposing regions in which there is not even the shadow of a central power. Agustín Gamarra is impersonated in the presidency of the Republic. After fulfilling his obscure period, he leaves power to General Orbegoso, an insignificant landowner of Trujillo. But the new president is immediately seized by Gamarra at the same time that General Felipe Santiago Salaverry is blindly launched to the conquest of power. The three proclaim themselves presidents of Peru. At that moment a soldier, Andrés Santa Cruz, whom Bolivar had made general by his action in the battle of Pichincha next to Sucre, presided over the Republic of Bolivia. Nevertheless, it is the man who, having contributed to the rupture of Bolivarian unity, proposes to remake it between Bolivia and Peru. Invited by President Orbegoso to contribute to the public order in Peru, convulsed by the military revolts, Santa Cruz is finally resolved, called by the Peruvian Congress, to enter with his troops to Peru. He fights with Salaverry, defeats him and shoots him,

---

incluyó, finalmente, gran parte de la zona occidental de los actuales estados de California, Texas, Nuevo México, Arizona, Utah, Nevada y parte de Colorado, pertenecientes a Estados Unidos desde 1848 [The Federal Republic of Central America was part of the viceroyalty of New Spain established in 1535. Its territory covered a large area whose natural center would be the valley of Mexico. On the foundations of the monumental <u>Tenochtitlan</u> was erected the city of Mexico, seat of the virreinal court during all the colonial period. The limits of the viceroyalty encompassed all of Central America (Guatemala, El Salvador, Nicaragua, Honduras, and Costa Rica), except for the governorship of Castilla de Oro with the strategic city of Panama. To the east, it included the Gulf of Mexico and the Caribbean Sea. However, the island territory composed of the small and large Antilles (Cuba, Santo Domingo and Puerto Rico among others), was not part of New Spain, constituting independent governorates. To the north, New Spain's jurisdiction eventually included much of the western part of the present-day states of California, Texas, New Mexico, Arizona, Utah, Nevada, and part of Colorado, which belonged to the United States since 1848].

expels Gamarra and forms the Peruvian-Bolivian Confederation. The news of the Confederation shook the political system of South America; before Chile and before the Argentine Confederation.[76] The common history of Lower and Upper Peru, their racial, historical, linguistic, and economic analogies made political unity a necessary outcome. On the other hand, Santa Cruz had been President of Peru and Marshal of his armed forces. But separatist factors began to rapidly undermine the confederal construction. The main enemy of the Confederation turned out to be the dictator of Chile, Diego Portales, representative of that rancid combination of merchants and conservative landowners who was the Chilean ruling class. He himself was a merchant of Valparaiso, the foreign port par excellence of Chile, the Buenos Aires of the Pacific. The reformulation of the Peru-Bolivian Confederation meant, among other things, making the port of Callao a more important port in the Pacific trade than that of Valparaíso. In this way, Portales rejects all proposals of the Bolivian to negotiate and declares war on the Confederation. But in addition to Portales, there was another Canning Creole from the burlesque South American balance on the other side of the Atlantic. It was Juan Manuel de Rosas. The prospect of a Peru-Bolivian Confederation, whose example could awaken the old links of the Argentine North with the provinces of Upper Peru, would bring serious problems to the hegemonic power that Rosas intended to maintain over the remaining provinces. Although Rosas refused to organize the United Provinces constitutionally, in order not to surrender the customs resources of Buenos Aires to a national power, neither was he willing to allow that Santa Cruz could eventually attract the bosom of his Confederation to some provinces of the Argentine North, fed

---

(76) Hugo Guerra Báez, **Portales y [and] Rosas**, p. 176, Ed. del Pacífico [Pacific Edition]; Santiago de Chile, 1958. Importa señalar que a Santa Cruz lo apoyan el Sur de Perú y Bolivia; pero el Norte Limeño y virreinal, siempre fue hostil al mestizo Serrano [It is important to note that Santa Cruz is supported by Southern Peru and Bolivia; But the northern Limeño and vice-regal, was always hostile to the half-blooded Serrano].

by Buenos Aires centralism. The Chilean troops invaded Peru accompanied by the General Agustín Gamarra and other Peruvian generals opposed to the Confederation. The diplomatic and military maneuvers of the astute Santa Cruz are rendered useless by the vastness of the Chilean and Peruvian forces[77] that unite against the Confederation. Santa Cruz leaves Lima and Gamarra proclaims himself President of Peru. At that time there are seven Presidents in Peru: Orbegoso, Gamarra, Santa Cruz, Riva, Aguero, Pio Tristán, Nieto and Vidol.[78] Shortly after, Santa Cruz is undone in the battle of Yungay by the Chilean General Manuel Bulnes. Simultaneously, the Vice-President of Bolivia, General Velasco, revolts against his chief in Tupiza and congratulates the Chilean Bulnes for his victory over the Confederation. On July 16, 1839, the "National" Congress was installed in Chuquisaca with the presidency of Jose Maria Serrano, unconditional of Santa Cruz and his policy until that moment. Serrano, however, struck Santa Cruz. The Congress declares *"Don Andrés Santa Cruz, President of Bolivia, an honorable traitor to the country, unworthy of the Bolivian name, erased from the civil and military lists of the Republic and outlawed from the moment he stepped on his territory"* [...].[79]

The Central American rupture with the Spanish metropolis happened in 1821. But the independence in Mexico derived towards the coronation like Emperor of the General Iturbide. The proximity of Guatemala and the ancient ties that both territories

---

(77) Rosas no pasó de provocar algunas escaramuzas en la frontera por medio del Gral. Heredia, Gobernador de Tucumán, y dejó morir de languidez su declaración de guerra [Rosas did not fail to provoke some skirmishes on the frontier through General Heredia, governor of Tucuman, and he let his declaration of war die of languor].

(78) Alfonso Crespo, **Santa Cruz**, Ed. Fondo de Cultura Económica [Fund of Economic Culture Edition], p. 284; México, 1944.

(79) Ibid., p. 321.

maintained suggested to Iturbide the idea of annexing Central America. The rupture of this violent bond, not accepted by all Central American provinces, came with the fall of the ephemeral Mexican Empire and the Central American Congress of 1823, which declared the political independence of Spain as well as of Mexico. From that date the old Kingdom of Guatemala began to be called United Provinces of Central America. The same Congress called for an Assembly to form a Confederation to represent the great American family. The inspirer of the idea was the Honduran Jose Cecilio del Valle, the most notable intellectual figure of independence. General Francisco de Morazán was given the task of launching the Federal Republic of Central America. He ruled that region for eight years and influenced Central America for nearly two decades. He was the most notable political and military figure of the period, but his program had to be developed in an incessant struggle against the factions of Central American separatism that subjected the unified Republic to a civil war without barracks. The separatist politics of the small regional politicians found an interested support in the British diplomatic intrigues. Complicated the goal of the federal union with the artificial antagonism between Catholics and liberals, the driving force of separatism was undoubtedly the same as in the rest of Hispanic America. In fact, as in San Salvador, since the last colonial days the powerful indigo producers were the most important political factor of that province, in the other tiny states export-import interests were grouped under the most diverse policies to impose their privileges linked to the world market. In 1837 Rafael Carrera conquers Guatemala and separates it from the Central American Union. The dissolution of the Federal Republic of Central America in 1838 was formalized when the Federal Congress declared that *"States are free to constitute themselves in whatever manner they deem appropriate".*[80] The loss of Guatemala undoes the Confederation.

---

(80) V. Ricardo Gallardo, **Las Constituciones de la República Federal de Centro-América [The Constitutions of the Federal Republic of Central America],**

El Salvador, Honduras, Nicaragua and Costa Rica are small republican states. Except in Costa Rica, where the expansion of coffee is beginning, little has changed in these depopulated corners of the Spanish empire. In Guatemala, Carrera's dominion that lasted until his death in 1865 lasted for thirty years, stimulating the remaining four states to their permanent division. In 1849 a new attempt of union was made under the name of National Representation of Central America, before the threat of a foreign imperialist intervention: the filibusters in the service of the United States sowed the alarm in Central America. Great Britain, on one hand, intended to extend its influence in the territories Mosquitos, belonging to Nicaragua and Honduras, through the artificial creation of the Mosquitia monarchy. Again in 1852, in Honduras, with the opposition of Carrera, an attempt was made for a national meeting constituent of Central America. The military campaigns of the other States of the time to overthrow Carrera and to impose the unity of the Isthmus failed, because the greatest economic power exporter of Central America resided in Guatemala, whose landlord class supported Carrera. At the same time, Costa Rica quarreled with Nicaragua over territorial issues over their respective rights in the Guanacaste region, border wounds deepened and poisoned by the English Consul Chatfield, which at that time promoted a blockade of Salvadoran ports with the argument of certain debts. Guatemala lost, under such circumstances (1851), the territory of Belize, which passed into the hands of England, nevertheless, that the latter supported Carrera without a cover. Between the United States and England, Central America was torn apart. While England renounced its alleged rights to the future Canal in the Isthmus, in favor of the United States, the latter permitted, in exchange, that England would increase its territory of Belize three times. President Carrera signed a monstrous treaty with England by which he ceded to the latter the territory of Belize, in exchange for the construction of a road from Guatemala City

Instituto de Estudios Políticos [Institute of Political Studies], p. 268; Madrid, 1958.

to the Atlantic coast. The road was never built, but England did not return Belize.[81]

Once Carrera was killed, General Justo Rufino Barrios assumed power of Guatemala in 1873. He was a nationalist liberal, resolute supporter of Central American unity. The General Barrios issued a Decree of Union on February 28, 1875 declaring the creation of a single Republic of Central America and assuming the character of Supreme Military Chief of the Nation. With this bismarkian coup, Barrios aspired to cut the secular serpent of discord from a single cut. But all the Central American governments opposed a union by force and demanded before the foreign governments in particular before Mexico, governed by the despot Porfirio Diaz. He responded by mobilizing the Mexican army to the Guatemalan border. At his meeting on March 19, 1885, the United States Senate declared that *"any attempt to forcibly join forces with the other Central American Republics would consider it an unfriendly and hostile intervention in their rights, pending the treaty on Interoceanic Canal"*.[82] The military actions concluded with the defeat of

---

(81) Jorge Abelardo Ramos, Ob. Cit., pp. 340-341. Belice era una fuente de pingues beneficios para Gran Bretaña, pues los leñadores ingleses cortaban palo campeche o palo Brasil, que obtenían altas cotizaciones en el mercado mundial. La codicia británica por Belice se remontaba al siglo XVIII. Los ingleses habían poblado ese territorio guatemalteco con negros y zambos originarios de Jamaica, entre ellos muchos condenados a presidio. El corte de palo de campeche era la actividad principal de los leñadores, al mando de británicos. Un siglo antes de la independencia se llegó a exportar hasta 5,800 toneladas de palo de campeche por año. La tonelada se pagaba en esa época hasta 100 libras esterlinas [Belize was a source of great benefits for Great Britain, as the English loggers cut Campeche wood or Brazilian wood, which obtained high prices in the world market. British greed for Belize dates back to the eighteenth century. The English had populated that Guatemalan territory with Negroes and Zambians from Jamaica, including many sentenced to prison. The cutting of Campeche wood was the main activity of the woodcutters, to the control of British. A century before the independence, up to 5,800 tons of campeche wood was exported per year. The ton was paid at that time up to 100 pounds sterling]. (Jorge Abelardo Ramos, Ob, cit., p. 341).

(82) V. Ricardo Gallardo, Ob. cit., p. 451

Barrios and with his own life in the battle of Chalchuapa. The rest of the attempts at Central American union belong more to the history of legal literature than to history itself. The United States, like England once, was opposed to all Latin American unity. To these frustrated attempts to build a Central American unitary state in the nineteenth century, the successive and regular invasions and occupations of Yankee marines will continue in the twentieth century. They will thus acquire the status of "occupied territories" - Nicaragua, Santo Domingo and Cuba - and forge the European tradition of "Banana Republics".

The violent struggle for the national unification of Latin America had thus ended, with the fall of Artigas, San Martin, Bolivar, Santa Cruz, Morazan and Barrios; Had lasted half a century. The last echoes of that struggle would manifest themselves in the field of politics and diplomacy in the rest of the nineteenth century. But the trend is declining. From unity through arms, it will pass to weak skirmishes through diplomacy. And just as Bolivarian unity has succeeded the subsequent fragmentation into "small republics" (as Bolivar called these aborted states), now will follow the territorial mutilation (Mexico) and even the cynical creation of elaborate states (Panama).

The program that Bolivar had begun in Panama in 1826 was to be completed in 1903, also in Panama, converted from cradle to grave of the Bolivarian flag. In order to build the Interoceanic Canal against the will of the Colombian Senate after the rejection of the Herran-Hay Treaty, the American government, relying on the Isthmian commercial lumpen-bourgeoisie, snatched its northern province from Colombia and announced to the World the birth of a new "sovereign" state.

V. THE NATURE OF STATES IN LATIN AMERICA

1. A FALSE CONCEPTION OF THE STATE IN LATIN AMERICA

The real difficulty when it comes to analyzing the essence of the state in Latin America, is that it does not arise from the unintelligence of the State as such, that is, the State as an instrument of class domination, but of the incapacity or ambiguity that Latin American thought has revealed to be specific, first, the **nature** and **specific social** classes that gave birth to it; Second, to problematize, in its right dimension, the functionality or dysfunctionality of the **nation** issue.

A strange coincidence of Latin American scholars has instituted as axiomatic postulate a generalized opinion in regional thinking. This view holds that the states that emerged from the struggles for independence in Latin America were established, organized and consolidated as nation states. Almost all historical, economic, political and sociological con ceptions, no matter what the ideological orientation of their authors converge on this point.

"In the first half of the nineteenth century, for example, Furtado is distinguished in Latin America by the struggles for independence and by the process of formation of national states".[1] The same author, entitled "From the Conquest to the Formation of the National States", the first part of

---

(1) Celso Furtado, **La Economía Latinoameicana desde la Conquista Ibérica hasta la Revolución Cubana [The Latin American Economy from the Iberian Conquest to the Cuban Revolution],** Ed. Universitaria [University Edition]; p. 3; Santiago, Chile, 1969.

his work, **The Latin American Economy from the Iberian conquest to the Cuban revolution**. *[...] "A good part of the nineteenth century," Sunkel and Paz add, "was a period during which the National States in Latin America were established, organized, and consolidated".[2] This conception is also shared by Latin American Marxists, some of them from ECLAC. "The perspective adopted in this essay," the authors of* **Dependence and Development in Latin America** *point out, "requires analyzing both the conditions and possibilities for development and consolidation of Latin American national states according to how local social groups manage to establish their participation in the productive process and managed to define forms of institutional control capable of securing it".[3] "The process of formation of the national state," Torres Rivas points out, "as a political project to reconstitute colonial power, fragmented by post-independence civil war and weakened by the absence of an internal market economy, is the starting point for the explanation of the power and politics in Central America".[4] "Formed as national states in the context of the crisis of the colonial system and in the context of the emergence of a new system of international domination," emphasizes Weffort, "the Latin American countries are originally and constitutively dependent".[5] [...] "The Constitution of the*

---

(2) Osvaldo Sunkel con colaboración de [with collaboration of] Pedro Paz, **El Subdesarrollo latinoamericano y la Teoría del Desarrollo [Latin American Underdevelopment and Development Theory]**; Siglo XXI [21st Century], 1a. Ed., p. 314; México, 1970.

(3) Fernando Henrique Cardoso y Enzo Faletto, **Dependencia y Desarrollo en América Latina [Dependence and Development in Latin America]**. (Ensayo de interpretación sociológica [Essay on sociological interpretation]); Siglo XXI [21st Century], 6a. Ed. p. 39; México, 1972.

(4) Edelberto Torres Rivas, *Síntesis histórica del proceso político [Historical synthesis of the political process];* en **Centroamérica hoy** [in **Central America today**]; Siglo XXI [21st Century], 2a. Ed., p. 12; México, 1976.

(5) Fco. C. Weffort, *Clases Populares y Desarrollo Social [Popular Classes and Social Development]*, en **Populismo, Marginación y dependencia** [In **Pop-**

National States," adds Cardoso, "has to be historically and structurally referred to both the liberalism of the first phase of industrial capitalist expansion and the symbiosis between the Privatist interests and bureaucratic-state interests that the previous expansion constituted since the colonial period".[6]
"The pampas bourgeoisie and its urban extensions," O'Donnell says, "were directly linked to the National State, not the regional state, which in the rest of Latin America was so often the main sphere of political power of the respective classes Dominant".[7] *"With Miter," adds Cortes Conde, "the foundations of a national state that would be definitively organized during the Roca era were laid".*[8] *"The development of dependent capitalism in each Latin American country, says Arnaldo Córdova, is intimately related to development of the national state and with its unifying action of national societies".*[9]

---

ulism, Marginalization and dependence] (ensayos de interpretación sociológica [Essays on sociological interpretation]), EDUCA; 1a. Ed. p. 39; Costa Rica, 1973.

(6) Fernando Henrique Cardoso, *Notas sobre el Estado actual de los Estudios sobre la dependencia [Notes on the Current Status of Dependency Studies]*, en **Desarrollo latinoamericano [In Latin American Development]** (ensayos críticos [Critical tests]), Selección de [Selections of] José Serra, F.C.E., 1a. Ed.; pp. 353-354; México, 1974.

(7) Guillermo O'Donnell, *Estado y Argentina, [State and Argentina] 1956-1976.* Documento [Document] CEDES/G.E.CLACSO/No. 5, presentado en el Symposium sobre **Estado y Desarrollo en América Latina** [Presented at the Symposium on **State and Development in Latin America**], Universidad de Cambridge [University of Cambridge], p. 9; 12—16 de diciembre de [The 12th — the 16th of December] 1976; Buenos Aires, octubre [October] 1976 (mimeo).

(8) Roberto Cortés Conde, *Problemas del crecimiento industrial de Argentina [Problems of industrial growth in Argentina]*, en la revista **Desarrollo Económico [In the Economic Development** magazine], No. **12**; Vol. [Volume] 3; abril-septiembre [April-September], 1963.

(9) Agustín Cueva, Arnaldo Córdova, Clodomiro Almeyda, Ruy Mauro Marini, Sergio Bagú, *El Estado en América Latina [The State in Latin America]* (mesa redonda [round table]), en **Revista Mexicana de Ciencias Políticas y Sociales [In Mexican Journal of Political and Social Sciences]**, (F.C.P.S., UNAM) No. 82; p. 14; octubre—diciembre [October-December], 1975.

[...] "In Chile," says Almeyda, "unlike other Latin American countries, the armed forces did not play a decisive and essential role in the Constitution of the National State "[10] "It is true that countries like Chile," observes Agustín Cueva, "and soon afterwards Uruguay, Costa Rica and Argentina succeeded in overcoming their period of 'anarchy' and consolidating relatively stable and homogeneous national states".[11] "As an ascending class (the landowner class -JETA-) made the country's independence in 1882 and organized the national state".[12] "From the end of the eighteenth century until the second third of the nineteenth century," Soler says, "it was the task of giving direction and sense to the formation of the different Spanish-American national states".[13]

Well, this uncontroversial axiomatic postulate seems to me absolutely questionable. Moreover, it has prevented, in my view, the elaboration of an adequate, theoretically fertile and politically effective explanation of the question of the State in Latin America.

To admit that the states that emerged from independence were constituted and organized as **National states** means to recognize, with all its implications, that in the first half of the nineteenth century the historical process of the formation of the **Nation** had been **consolidated** in Latin America, that is

---

(10) Ibid., p. 22.

(11) Ibid., pp. 42-43.

(12) Guerrero Ramos, *A dinámica da sociedade política no Brasil [The dynamics of political society in Brazil]*, **Revista Brasileira de Estudos Políticos [Brazilian Journal of Political Studies]**, No. 1, p. 30; dezembro de [December] 1956.

(13) Ricaurte Soler, *La Independencia de Panamá de Colombia (Sobre el problema nacional hispanoamericano) [The Panama Independence of Colombia (On the National Hispanic American Problem)]*, en revista **Tareas** [in **Task** magazine] No. 25, p, 94; Panamá, noviembre 1972-mayo 1973 [November 192 – May 1973].

to say That "nations," as Ricaurte Soler asserts, ***"pre-exist the
formation** of an industrial bourgeoisie and the consolidation
of the capitalist mode of production",*[14] or accept with Samir
Amin that [...] *"the nation is a social phenomenon that can
appear in all The stages of history, and that is not necessary or
exclusively correlative to the mode of capitalist production"*
[...].[15] And to admit such positions would be not only to quar-
rel with the historical reality of the Continent but to invalidate
the solidly elaborated and historically confirmed thesis of the
national question in Marxism-Leninism.

Let's take a closer look at the problem.

2. THE NATION AND THE FORMATION OF THE NATIONAL STATES IN EUROPE IN THE EIGHTEENTH AND NINETEENTH CENTU-RIES. PARTICULARITY IN THE CASE OF LA-TIN AMERICAN COUNTRIES.

*"Nation," says Stalin, "is a human community, stable,
historically formed and based on the community of language, territory, economic life and psychology, manifest this
in the community of culture".*[16]

---

(14) Ricaurte Soler, Ob. cit., p. 96.

(15) Samir Amin, **Categorías y Leyes fundamentales del capitalismo [Cate-
gories and fundamental laws of capitalism]**; Ed. Nuestro Tiempo [Our Time
Edition]; 2a. Ed., p. 31; México, 1975.

(16) J. V. Stalin, *El marxismo y la cuestión nacional [Marxism and the national
question],* en **Obras Completas** en 17 Tomos [in **Complete Works** in 17 Vol-
umes]; Edit. Actividad EDA [EDA Activity Editorial]; 1a. Ed.; Tomo 2 [Volume
II]; p. 316; México, 1977. Cursivas de Stalin [Stalin Italics].

*"It is understood that the nation, like all historical phenomena, is subject to the law of change, has its history, its beginning and its end. It is necessary to underline," Stalin adds, "that none of the features indicated, taken in isolation, is enough to define the nation, and even if it is one of these traits, so that the nation ceases to be. **It is only the joint presence of all the distinctive features that forms the nation**".[17]*

Despite Michael Lówy's claims, this was, no doubt, the conception of Lenin and of the "Bolshevik" party he headed.[18]

----

(17) Ibid., pp. 316-317. Cursivas de Stalin [Stalin Italics].

(18) "Del famoso artículo de Stalin 'El Marxismo y la Cuestión Nacional'; es cierto —sostiene Lówy— que fue Lenin quien mandó a Stalin a Viena a escribirlo[...]..Pero una vez que el artículo estuvo terminado, pareció (contrariamente al mito popular) que Lenin no estaba particularmente entusiasmado con él, ya que no lo menciona en ninguno de sus numerosos escritos sobre la cuestión nacional, aparte de una corta referencia de pasada y entre paréntesis, en un artículo fechado el 28 de diciembre de 1913[...]..En un cierto número de puntos medianamente importantes del trabajo de Stalin —subraya—, difiere, implícita y explícitamente, e incluso contradice los escritos de Lenin [...]Por la sencilla razón de que 'es sólo cuando todas estas características (lenguaje común, territorio, vida económica y formación síquica) están presentes juntas que tenemos una nación', Stalin dio a su teoría un carácter dogmático restrictivo y rígido que uno nunca encuentra en Lenin[...]En ninguna parte de los escritos de Lenin -agrega- encontramos una 'definición' de nación tan primaria, rígida y arbitraria [From Stalin's famous article 'Marxism and the National Question', it is true, says Lówy, that it was Lenin who sent Stalin to Vienna to write it [...] But once the article was finished, it seemed (contrary to popular myth) That Lenin was not particularly enthusiastic about him, since he did not mention it in any of his numerous writings on the national question, apart from a brief reference in passing and in parentheses, in an article dated December 28, 1913 [...] In a number of very important points of Stalin's work, he points out, it differs, implicitly and explicitly, and even contradicts Lenin's writings [...] For the simple reason that 'it is only when all these characteristics (common language, territory, life Economic and psychic formation) are present together that we have a nation,' Stalin gave his theory a restrictive and rigid dogmatic character that one never finds in Lenin [...] Nowhere in Lenin's writings - he adds - we find a 'definition' Of a nation so primitive, rigid and arbitrary]". (Michael Lowy, *Los marxistas y la cuestión nacional* [*Marxists and the national question*], en la revista **Ideología y Sociedad** [In the magazine **Ideology and Society**], Bogotá, Colombia, enero-marzo de [January-March] 1977, pp. 22-23). Esta posición de Michael Lowy nos parece equivocada. En primer lugar, no es correcto afirmar que en un cierto número de puntos medianamente importantes el "trabajo de Stalin contradice los escritos de Lenin" y menos aún que éste "no estaba particularmente entusiasmado con él, ya que no lo menciona en ninguno de sus numerosos escritos sobre la

cuestión nacional". [...]El artículo "El Marxismo y la cuestión nacional" fue escrito a fines de 1912 y comienzos de 1913 en Viena. A propósito del artículo, en febrero (nuevo cómputo) de 1913 Vladimir Ilich escribía a A.M. Gorki: "Entre nosotros se halla ahora un maravilloso georgiano que está escribiendo un extenso artículo para **Prosveschenie**. A este fin ha reunido todos los materiales austríacos y otros [This position of Michael Lowy seems wrong to us. First, it is not correct to say that in a number of moderately important points Stalin's "work" contradicts Lenin's writings, let alone that "he was not particularly enthusiastic about it, since he does not mention it in any of his numerous writings on the national question". [...] The article "Marxism and the national question" was written in late 1912 and early 1913 in Vienna. Regarding the article, in February (re-count) of 1913 Vladimir Ilyich wrote to A.M. Gorky: "Among us is now a wonderful Georgian who is writing an extensive article for **Prosveschenie**. To this end he has gathered all the Austrian and other materials]". (Nota del archivo del Instituto Marx-Engels-Lenin [Note from the archive of the Marx-Engels-Lenin Institute], en [in] J.V. Stalin, Ob. cit., p. 429). En 1913 se publicó por primera vez, con la firma de K. Stalin [In 1913 it was first published, with the signature of. K. Stalin], en los números 3, 4 y 5 de la revista **Prosveschenie** [In numbers 3, 4 and 5 of **Prosveschenie** magazine], con el título *La cuestión nacional y la social-democracia [With the title The national question and the social-democracy]*. Más aún, al saber que se pensaba estimar el artículo de J.V. Stalin como artículo de discusión, Lenin se opuso de manera resuelta: "Como es natural, nosotros estamos absolutamente en contra. El artículo es **muy bueno**. La cuestión es batallona y no cederemos ni una pulgada de nuestras posiciones de principio frente a la canalla bundista [Moreover, on learning that it was intended to estimate the article of J.V. Stalin as a discussion article, Lenin resolutely opposed: "Naturally, we are absolutely against it, the article is **very good**, the issue is battalion and we will not give an inch of our positions of principle in front of the bundista scoundrel]". (Ibid., p. 429). Por otra parte, al poco de la detención de J.V. Stalin, en marzo de 1913, V.I. Lenin escribía a la redacción de **Sotsial-Demokrat**: [...] "Hemos sufrido detenciones dolorosas. Han detenido a Koba[...] Antes de su detención ha podido escribir un extenso artículo (para tres números de **Prosveschenie**) sobre la cuestión nacional. ¡Muy bien! Hay que combatir por la verdad contra los separatistas y oportunistas del Bund y de los liquidadores" [On the other hand, shortly after the arrest of J.V. Stalin, March 1913, V.I. Lenin wrote to the editors of **Sotsial-Demokrat**: "We have suffered painful arrests and have arrested Koba [...] Before his arrest he was able to write an extensive article (for three issues of **Prosveschenie**) on the national question. We must fight for the truth against the separatists and opportunists of the Bund and the liquidators]" (Ibid., p. 429). En 1914 el artículo de J.V. Stalin fue publicado en folleto aparte, bajo el título de "La cuestión nacional y el marxismo" por la Edit. **Priboi** de Petersburgo. El hecho de que Lenin no se refiriera en sus numerosos escritos posteriores sobre la cuestión al trabajo de Stalin se explica precisamente en esa "corta referencia de pasada" a la que hace mención Lowy. En el artículo "acerca del programa nacional del P.O.S.D.R.", (escrito el 28 de diciembre de 1913) Lenin señalaba: "En esta resolución se indica en detalle por qué y de qué modo el problema nacional ha pasado a ocupar hoy un lugar destacado tanto en toda la política de la contrarrevolución y en la conciencia de clase de la burguesía, como en el partido proletario socialdemócrata de Rusia. **En verdad no creemos que haya necesidad de pararse a tratar** de ello ya que los términos de la cuestión están completamente claros. En la literatura teórica marxista, esta cuestión y las bases del programa nacional social demócrata han sido esclarecidas en el último tiempo. (Se alude a la obra de J.V. Stalin "El marxismo y el problema nacional[...]Por eso estimamos que en el presente artículo (y en los sucesivos –JETA-) será oportuno limitarse a plantear el problema desde un punto de vista puramente partidista y explicar lo que la prensa legal, oprimida por el yugo de Stolypin-Maklakov, no puede decir** [In 1914 the article of J.V. Stalin was published in a separate pamphlet, under the title "The National Question and Marxism" by Edit. **Priboi** from Petersburg. The fact that Lenin did not refer in his many later writings on the question to Stalin's work is explained precisely in that "short pass reference" to which Lowy mentions. In the article "on the national program of the RSDLP" (written on December 28, 1913), Lenin stated: "This resolution indicates in detail why and how the national problem has now become so prominent in all the politics of the counterrevolution and in the class consciousness of the bourgeoisie, as in the proletarian social-democratic party of Russia, **we do not really believe that there is any need to stop to deal with it, since the terms of the question are completely clear. In Marxist theoretical literature, this question and the bases of the national democratic social program have been clarified in the last time. (It is alluded to the work of JV Stalin "Marxism and the national problem [...] That is why we consider that in this article and in the subsequent -JETA-) it would be appropriate to confine itself to raising the problem from a purely partisan point of view and explaining what the legal press, oppressed by Stolypin-Maklakov's yoke, cannot say]".** (V.I. Lenin, *Acerca del programa nacional del P.O.S.D.R. [About the national program of P.O.S.D.R]*, en **Obras Completas** [In **Complete Works**], Editorial Cartago [Carthage Editorial], tomo XIX [Volume XIX], p. 533, Buenos Aires, 1960) Cursivas de JETA [JETA Italics]. En cuanto a la afirmación de Lowy de que "Stalin dio a su teoría un carácter dogmático, restrictivo y rígido que uno nunca encuentra en Lenin", por el hecho de que Stalin subraye que **"sólo la presencia conjunta de todos los rasgos distintivos forman la nación",** [As for Lowy's assertion that "Stalin gave his theory a dogmatic, restrictive and rigid character that one never finds in Lenin", because Stalin stresses that **"only the joint presence of all distinctive features form the Nation,"** también nos parece errónea, pues éstos son los elementos que constituyen la esencia de la nación como fenómeno y es lógico y natural que al faltar uno solo de estos rasgos la nación deje de serlo. Lo mismo ocurriría si alteráramos la esencia de cualquier sustancia química. Si por ejemplo a $H2O$ le elimináramos la molécula de oxigeno, el agua dejaría de serlo; si de $H2O2$ separamos una molécula de oxigeno, el agua oxigenada ($H2O2$) se convertiría en simple agua ($H2O$), es decir en una sustancia total y cualitativamente distinta. Por lo demás, [...] "la suge rencia de Trotsky -a la que se refiere Lowy- de que el artículo fue - inspirado, supervisado y corregido 'línea por línea' por Lenin, nos parece acertada[...] [also seems wrong to us, for these are the elements that constitute the essence of the nation as a phenomenon and it is logical and natural that when one of these traits fails, the nation ceases to be so. The same would happen if we alter the essence of any chemical substance. If, for example, $H2O$ were to remove the molecule of oxygen, water would cease to be; If $H2O2$ separates a molecule of oxygen, hydrogen

According to this conception, "the nation" is not simply a historical category, but a historical category of a certain epoch, of the epoch of ascensional capitalism. The process of liquidation of feudalism and development of capitalism is at the same time The British, the French, the Germans, the Italians, and so on, became nations under the triumphal march of victorious capitalism over the division feudal.

"But there," Stalin points out, "the formation of nations meant, at the same time, their transformation into independent national states. The English, French, and so on are at the same time English states, etc. ".[19]

Here arises the second great divergence with Ricaurte Soler, one of the few authors, who try to base theoretically the existence of Latin American nations and, therefore, of national States, during the nineteenth century.

From the reading of the earlier paragraphs of Stalin's work, particularly from the claim that "nation" is "a historical category" of the epoch of ascensional capitalism, Soler concludes:

*"It is clear, then, that national formation is inseparable from a certain period **of transition**: that which defines the process of liquidation of feudalism and the development of capitalism. In Latin America that transition, for the nations of lesser delay, extends from the late eighteenth century to the*

---

peroxide (H2O2) would become simple water (H2O), that is to say in a totally and qualitatively different substance. Otherwise [...] "Trotsky's suggestion," to which Lowy refers, "that the article was - inspired, supervised and corrected 'line by line' by Lenin, seems to us to be correct"]. (Trotsky, **Stalin**, Vol. I, p. 233, Londres 1969, citado por [cited by] Michael Lowy, Ob. cit., p. 22).

(19) J.V. Stalin, Ob. cit., p. 323.

second third of the nineteenth century".[20] In other words, for this author, "nations pre-exist the formation of an industrial bourgeoisie and the consolidation of the capitalist mode of production".[21]

This interpretation of Stalin, which serves as a theoretical foundation for the Solerian conception of the nation in Spanish America "from the end of the eighteenth century to the second third of the nineteenth century" and the formation of national states, seems to us to be absolutely wrong.

Soler himself falls into a contradiction, for he recognizes, on the one hand, that **the age of ascensional capitalism** corresponds to a certain period of transition: "that which defines the process of liquidation of feudalism and the development of capitalism," and, On the other hand, denies that this period is inseparable from the epoch of bourgeois revolutions in Western Europe, i.e., the triumph of the industrial bourgeoisie and the consolidation of the capitalist mode of production.

In this regard, Lenin is very clear.

"Throughout the world, the epoch of capitalism's definitive triumph over feudalism was linked to national movements. The economic basis of these movements is that, for the complete victory of mercantile production, it is necessary for the bourgeoisie to conquer the internal market"

[...] "In Western Europe, the continent of Europe," he adds later, "the epoch of bourgeois-democratic revolutions encompasses a fairly fixed period of time, roughly from 1789

---

(20) Ricaurte Soler, Ob. cit., p. 96.

(21) Ibid., p. 96.

to 1871. ***This was precisely the era of national movements and creation of national States.***[22]

Therefore, the process of historical culmination of the nation and the formation of national states in Western Europe corresponds, contrary to what Soler argues, to the era of bourgeois-democratic revolutions, that is, the triumph of the industrial bourgeoisie and the consolidation of capitalism. It is within this framework that the nation must be understood as a historical category of the era of ascensional capitalism. Soler's second erroneous statement is understood when he argues that for the less delayed "nations", his period of formation extends from the late eighteenth century to the second third of the nineteenth century, as well as the dysfunctionalness of the dogmatic principle, sustained In the region by all the currents of Latin American thought, that the states that emerged from independence were organized and consolidated as **National states**.

It is important to emphasize that the work of Cardoso and Faletto, **Dependence and Development in Latin America,** is one of the most expressive manifestations of the dogmatic form as this principle applies. Many of the positions of dependency theory, at least in the version of these authors, are based on the assumption of this axiomatic principle that underlies the whole conception of the State in Latin America.

[...]"The creation of national states, and the control of local economies," Cardoso and Faletto argue, "mean that associations of interests of economically oriented classes and groups establish forms of authority and power in such a way as

---

(22) V.I. Lenin, *Sobre el derecho de las naciones a la auto-determinación [On the right of nations to self-determinate]* en **Obras Escogidas** [In **Selected Works**] (en tres tomos [in three volumes]); Editorial Progreso [Progress Editorial], pp. 616 y 624; Moscú, 1966. (Cursivas de JETA [JETA Italics]).

to constitute a legitimate order."[23] [...] "The forms assumed by the relations between the economic system and the power system from the period of implementation of the independent national states," they assert later, "gave rise to different possibilities of development and autonomy for the Latin American countries, according to their peculiar situations"[24] _ "In order to understand the present situations, from which we depart, we point out, it requires analyze, however brief, of the historical situations that explain how the American nations are linked to the world system of Power and the periphery of the international economy".[25] [...] "The formation of nations in Latin America, they add, was made possible through local social groups whose capacity to structure a local system of political and economic control varied fairly according to the historical process of constitution in the colonial period".[26] [...] "Naturally, they say, the process of national formation could be more successful in the case of the colonies that had been organized as the agricultural base of the metropolitan economy."[27] "The rupture of the colonial pact and the formation of national states imply, therefore, a new way of ordering the economy and local society in Latin America".[28]

From there, the correctness of Lechner's statement when he notes that: "the study of Cardoso and Faletto starts from the establishment of an independent nation through anti-colonialist struggles. The existence of the nation, identified with the national state, is the starting point The nation does not

---

(23) Fernando Henrique Cardoso y [and] Enzo Faletto, Ob. cit., p. 39.

(24) Ibid., p. 39.

(25) Ibid., p. 40.

(26) Ibid., p. 40.

(27) Ibid., p. 41.

(28) Ibid., p. 42.

have the status of an explanatory category but rather names the universe of analysis". [29]

Having put it this way, it is not difficult to understand why some authors maintain that "theorizing about the State is a constituent part of the process of rupture with dependents conceptions, unable to account for political processes without falling into reductionism". [30]

The process of formation of the nation has not been consolidated in Latin America; The absence of a genuine industrial bourgeoisie is its legitimate explanation. Hence, the impossibility of National States in the nineteenth century and in the twentieth century; The Mexican industrial bourgeoisie that struggles to assert its national state could be the exception of the twentieth century in Mexico; however, it does not exist until today but an **Unfinished national state.** [31]

---

(29) Norbert Lechner, **La crisis del Estado en América Latina [The crisis of the state in Latin America]**, El Cid Editor [The Cid Editor]; p. 113; Caracas, 1977.

(30) Liliana de Riz, *Formas de Estado y Desarrollo del Capitalismo en América Latina*, en **Revista Mexicana de Sociología**, p.439; abril-junio de 1977.

(31) Este es el único país del Continente que logró realizar una revolución democrático-burguesa. El resto de los intentos de revoluciones burguesas antioligárquicas, anti-feudales y anti-imperialistas (Guatemala 1944, Bolivia 1952, República Dominicana 1965, Perú 1968, para citar algunos ejemplos), se frustraron. La revolución mexicana que se inicia en 1910 derrocó políticamente al sector tradicional y moderno de la oligarquía y destruyó, en gran parte, su base económica. El ascenso al poder de la burguesía industrial nacional fue configurando un poder exclusivo de esta clase, que alcanza su expresión política e institucional en el PRI (Partido Revolucionario Institucional). ¿En qué consiste, pues, la dificultad de la consolidación del Estado nacional mexicano si después del derrocamiento político del sector tradicional y moderno de la oligarquía, que trajo consigo la revolución de 1910, fue la burguesía industrial la que ascendió al poder? ¿Por qué designamos a este Estado como un Estado nacional inconcluso? "El capitalismo en desarrollo -decía Lenin- conoce dos tendencias históricas en el problema nacional. La primera consiste en el despertar de la vida nacional y de los movimientos nacionales, en la lucha contra toda opresión nacional, en la

creación de Estados nacionales. La segunda es el desarrollo y la multiplicación de vínculos de todas clases entre las naciones, la destrucción de las barreras nacionales, la formación de la unidad Ínter nacional del capital, de la vida económica en general, de la política, de la ciencia, etc. Ambas tendencias son una ley universal del capitalismo. La primera predomina en los comienzos de su desarrollo, la segunda distingue al capitalismo maduro que marcha hacia su trans formación en sociedad socialista [This is the only country on the Continent to achieve a bourgeois-democratic revolution. The rest of the attempts of anti-oligarchic, anti-feudal and anti-imperialist bourgeois revolutions (Guatemala 1944, Bolivia 1952, Dominican Republic 1965, Peru 1968, to name but a few) were frustrated. The Mexican revolution that began in 1910 politically overthrew the traditional and modern sector of the oligarchy and largely destroyed its economic base. The ascendancy to power of the national industrial bourgeoisie was configuring an exclusive power of this class, which reaches its political and institutional expression in the PRI (Partido Revolucionario Institucional). What, then, is the difficulty of the consolidation of the Mexican national state if, after the political overthrow of the traditional and modern sector of the oligarchy brought about by the revolution of 1910, it was the industrial bourgeoisie that rose to power? Why do we designate this State as an unfinished national State? "Developing capitalism," said Lenin, "knows two historical trends in the national problem: the first is the awakening of national life and national movements in the struggle against all national oppression in the creation of national states. Second is the development and multiplication of all kinds of ties between nations, the destruction of national barriers, the formation of the national unity of capital, of economic life in general, of politics, of science, and so on. Both tendencies are a universal law of capitalism, the former predominates at the beginning of its development, the second distinguishes the mature capitalism that marches towards its transformation into a socialist society]". (V.1. Lenin, *Notas críticas sobre el problema nacional [Critical Notes on the National Problem]*, en **Obras Completas** [In **Complete Works**], Editorial Cartago [Editorial Cartago], Tomo XX [Volume XX], pp. 26-27). Pues bien, el desarrollo de la burguesía industrial mexicana ocurre en la segunda fase del desarrollo capitalista, en la etapa de la destrucción de las barreras nacionales y de la formación de la unidad internacional del capital, es decir, en la época del imperialismo. Esto implica una fuerte penetración de capital foráneo y la vinculación con este capital de los sectores de la oligarquía moderna que fueron desalojados del poder político, como la desnacionalización de un sector significativo de la burguesía industrial-nacional. La división de la burguesía se expresa claramente en las organizaciones empresariales del país: CONCAMIN (Confederación de Cámaras Industriales), CONCANACO (Confederación de Cámaras de Comercio) y CANACINTRA (Cámara Nacional de la Industria de Transformación). El gobierno y los industriales nativos -sostenía Domingo Lavin, expresidente de la CANACINTRA en 1960 deben planear conjuntamente el desarrollo económico con el objetivo de asegurar el uso más efectivo del escaso capital disponible. En esta tarea de planificación se considera que la CANACIN-

TRA, como una organización que verdaderamente representa los grupos productivos, es a quien debe consultar el gobierno, en lugar de organizaciones como la CONCAMIN y la CONCANACO que no son representativas del punto de vista económico nacionalista [Well, the development of the Mexican industrial bourgeoisie occurs in the second phase of capitalist development, at the stage of the destruction of national barriers and the formation of the international unity of capital, that is, in the era of imperialism. This implies a strong penetration of foreign capital and the link with this capital of sectors of the modern oligarchy that were evicted from political power, such as the denationalization of a significant sector of the industrial-national bourgeoisie. The division of the bourgeoisie is clearly expressed in the country's business organizations: CONCAMIN (Confederation of Industrial Chambers), CONCANACO (Confederation of Chambers of Commerce) and CANACINTRA (National Chamber of the Transformation Industry). The government and native industrialists, Domingo Lavin, former president of CANACINTRA in 1960, must jointly plan economic development with the aim of ensuring the most effective use of scarce available capital. In this planning task, CANACINTRA, as an organization that truly represents productive groups, is considered by the government, instead of organizations such as CONCAMIN and CONCANACO, which are not representative of the nationalist economic point of view]. (José Domingo Lavin, **Siempre [Always]**, diciembre 21 de [December 21st] 1960). "Filosóficamente unidas a estas organizaciones," apunta Davis Bendecio, "surgió la Confederación de Centros Patronales que fue fundada por elemen tos disidentes cuando el gobierno obligó a todos los industriales y comerciantes a formar Cámaras. Estos elementos organizaron su Confederación de Centros Patronales en oposición a la intervención estatal en la industria bajo el General Cárdenas ["Philosophically united to these organizations," according to Davis Bendecio, "the Confederation of Employers' Centers emerged, which was founded by dissident elements when the government compelled all industrialists and traders to form Chambers, which organized their Confederation of Employers' Centers in opposition to intervention State in the industry under General Cardenas]". (Davis Bendecio, The position of CANACINTRA on foreign investment; Master's Essay, p. 7, Columbia University, New York, 1962). En 1960, el Gobierno amplió sus actividades en ciertos campos como la petroquímica y penetró en nuevas industrias que anteriormente eran de dominio exclusivo del capital privado y extranjero. Esta expansión de la actividad gubernamental provocó sentimientos adversos, particularmente de los opositores tradicionales al punto de vista de la CANACINTRA, la CONCANACO, la CONCAMIN y la Confederación de Centros Patronales de la República Mexicana. En noviembre de 1960, estas tres organizaciones publicaron conjuntamente un artículo titulado "¿Qué camino, Sr. Presidente?" "Este documento," afirma Bendecio, "contiene tres afirmaciones que definen su actitud: 1) el gobierno adquiere empresas con fondos que debieran utilizarse para obras públicas; 2) el gobierno está conduciendo al país al Socialismo de Estado; 3) estamos presenciando el principio de una nueva política económica contraria al sistema estable-

Let us see the particularity of the historical frustration of the nation in Latin America.

---

cido por la Ley de Propiedad Privada [...] libre empresa y responsabilidad pública [In 1960, the government expanded its activities in certain fields such as petrochemicals and penetrated new industries that were previously exclusively owned by private and foreign capital. This expansion of government activity provoked adverse feelings, particularly from traditional opponents to the point of view of CANACINTRA, CONCANACO, CONCAMIN and the Confederation of Employers' Centers of the Mexican Republic. In November 1960, these three organizations jointly published an article entitled "Which way, Mr. President?" "This document," says Bendecio, "contains three statements that define its attitude: (1) the government acquires companies with funds that should be used for public works, (2) the government is leading the country to state socialism, (3) A new economic policy contrary to the system established by the Law of Private Property [...] free enterprise and public responsibility]" (Revista **Mañana** [**Morning** Magazine], diciembre 3 de [December 3rd] 1960, p. 27; citado por [quoted by] Ibid., p. 17) "Está de más decir -agrega el autor-, que la actitud de la CANACINTRA fue absolutamente contraria a la expresada en ese documento y totalmente a favor de las acciones del gobierno en sus nuevas inversiones industriales ["It is an overstatement," adds the author, "that CANACINTRA's attitude was absolutely contrary to the one expressed in that document and totally in favor of the actions of the government in its new industrial investments]" (Ibid., p. 17). "La petición más reciente de la CONCAMIN, CONCANACO y la Confederación de Centros Patronales al Presidente ha sido diseñada para limitar y restringir las medidas importantes que el Presidente López Mateos ha estado tomando en interés del progreso de México ["The most recent petition of CONCAMIN, CONCANACO and the Confederation of Employers' Associations to the President has been designed to limit and restrict the important measures President López Mateos has been taking in the interest of Mexico's progress]" (José Domingo Lavin, "Contagio Mental de los Negociantes ["Mental Contagion of Traders]", **Siempre** [**Always**], diciembre 15 de [December 15th] 1960, p. 15). Esta división de la burguesía mexicana y la fuerte presión que ejerce la Confederación de Centros Patronales sobre la política económica del Estado, unida a la influencia notable de los Estados Unidos sobre la economía y por ende sobre la política mexicana, es lo que impide, en mi opinión, la consolidación del Estado nacional, la existencia de un Estado nacional inconcluso en México [This division of the Mexican bourgeoisie and the strong pressure exerted by the Confederation of Employers' Centers on the economic policy of the State, together with the notable influence of the United States on the economy and, consequently, on Mexican politics, is what, in my opinion, prevents the consolidation of the national state, the existence of an unfinished national state in Mexico].

Unlike Western Europe where the formation of nations meant at the same time their transformation into independent national states (The English, French nations, etc., are at the same time the English and French states, etc.). In East Europe, multinational states were formed, States formed by several nationalities. Such is the case of Austria-Hungary and Russia. In Austria, the most developed in the political sense turned out to be the Germans, and they assumed the task of unifying the Austrian nationalities in a State. In Hungary, the most suitable for the state organization turned out to be the Magyars - the nucleus of Hungarian nationalities - and they were the unifiers of Hungary. In Russia, the great Russians assumed the role of unifiers of the nationalities, at the head of which was a powerful and organized aristocratic military bureaucracy formed in the course of history.

"This peculiar mode of state formation," Stalin remarks, "could only take place under the conditions of a feudalism still unresolved under the conditions of a weakly developed capitalism in which the nationalities relegated to the background had not yet been able to consolidate themselves economically as Integral nations". [32]

Well, in Latin America neither one nor the other happened; Nor the formation of national States, nor the formation of multinational States, although here, from the point of view of what Samir Amin understands by **ethnicity**, conditions much more favorable than in Western Europe for the formation of the **nation** and , Therefore, of **National States**.

"Ethnicity" and obviously not race "supposes a linguistic and cultural community and homogeneity of the geographical

---

(32) J.V. Stalin, Ob., cit., p. 324.

*territory and above all the awareness of this cultural homo-
geneity".* [33]

In Latin America, all these essential elements of the determination of the nation were concentrated, in general terms and at the Continental level. Moreover, we had a clear awareness of our linguistic, geographical and cultural unity, which was expressed in the Bolivarian ideology. The intelligence of that conscience fought actively, with arms and diplomacy, for that sublime ideal of the Confederation of Spanish American States.

*"The association of the five States of America," Bolivar
wrote to O'Higgins, "is so sublime in itself that I am sure it
will be a source of astonishment for Europe".* [34]

---

(33) Samir Amin, Ob. cit., p. 30. "La nación -apunta este autor- supone la etnia pero la rebasa. ¿En qué? La nación aparece si además, una clase social que controle el aparato central del estado, asegura una unidad económica a la vida de la comunidad. Esta definición es más amplia que la basada sobre el mercado capitalista; la clase en cuestión no es necesaria y exclusivamente la burguesía ["The nation" this author points out "supposes the ethnicity but it surpasses it. In which? The nation appears if, in addition, a social class that controls the central apparatus of the state, assures an economic unit to the life of the community. This definition is broader than that based on the capitalist market; The class in question is not necessarily and exclusively the bourgeoisie]". (Ibid. p. 30). "Es a Zahrane -anota Samir Amin- a quien debemos esta idea de que el fenómeno nacional debe ser asociado a la existencia de una clase que asegura la unidad económica del país, y esta unidad económica debe ser entendida en sentido más amplio que el que procede del mercado capitalista ["It is to Zahrane," said Samir Amin, "to whom we owe this idea that the national phenomenon must be associated with the existence of a class which assures the economic unity of the country, and this economic unity must be understood in a broader sense than that which comes from the capitalist market] (ibid., p. 148). Naturalmente que esta concepción, por razones obvias, es mucho menos avanzada que la que sostiene Soler [Naturally, this conception, for obvious reasons, is much less advanced than that which Soler maintains].

(34) Bolivar, *Documentos [Documents]*, p. 107, Ed. Casa de las Américas [House of the Americas Edition], La Habana [Havana].

An idea that took shape in the Amphictyonic Congress of Panama; which was unanimously approved on July 15, 1826: the "Treaty of Union League and perpetual Confederation between the Republics of Peru, Colombia, Central America and United Mexican States".

We had, therefore, propitious, historical and geographical-natural conditions, and a clear political conscience to form a single Latin American nation with solid national states. However, the historical reality was another: balkanization in "sovereign republics" and absence of national States, that is to say, a nation unfinished with frustrated national States.

The only explanation for this historical truth is to carouse it, in my opinion, the absence of an industrial bourgeoisie in the nineteenth century and its authenticity in the twentieth century. Hence, the correctness of Stalin's assertion when he maintained that *[...]* *"none of the indicated features, taken in isolation, is sufficient to define the nation [...] It is enough that one of these traits is missing, so that the nation ceases to be so".* [35]

The states that emerged in Latin America after independence were organized and consolidated as instruments of the Latin American **oligarchies**. Sometimes as an expression of the **traditional oligarchy** (the case, of the Mexican State until the triumph of liberalism with Juarez, or of the Brazilian state of the Empire era); Others as a form of domination of the **modern oligarchy** (the Argentine state throughout the nineteenth century and practically until the triumph of radicalism); And not infrequently as an instrument of the alliance between the **modern oligarchy and the traditional oligarchy** (the Mexican State of the Porfiriato, or the Brazilian State of the First Republic). As an expression of the **traditional oligar-**

---

(35) J. V. Stalin, Ob., cit., p. 316.

chy, the **oligarchic state** defended the interests of the **conservatives**, that is, of the great feudal or semi-feudal aristocracy; As a form of domination of the **modern oligarchy** was always an oligarchic state at the service of **liberalism** (of the importing merchants and the export bourgeoisie). From this perspective, the triumph of **liberalism** in Latin America was the triumph of the **modern oligarchic state**, and its purest expression the nineteenth-century Argentine state. Where the defeat of the Conservatives was the result of a long civil war, the modern oligarchic state was not configured with the **exclusive** dominance of the **liberals**, but with a strong participation of the conservatives; we have already cited the example of the Porfirist State.

Therefore, the states that emerged in Latin America after the independence were organized and consolidated as oligarchic states. And because the classes that served as support for these States were not linked to the internal market, that is to say, interested in the development of industrial capitalism, oligarchic states were always, by their very nature, antinational and foreign.

These classes denied and destroyed all the favorable conditions for the development of capitalism which were present in the continent.

[...] "Capitalism," Lenin points out, "requires for its development States that are the most extensive and most centralized [...] There is no doubt," he adds, "that the homogeneous national composition of the population is one of the most favorable factors for a free economic exchange, broad and truly modern [...] One can be assured, in this sense, that among the modern demands of capitalism will be that of the maximum national homogeneity of the population, since nationality, language identity, is an important factor for the full conquest

*of the internal market and for the complete freedom of eco-
nomic exchange".*[36]

In Latin America, as we have already indicated, all these
factors occurred, and yet the results were reversed: fragmentation of Latin American unity and full liberalism against the
nascent national manufacturing.

This is another way of explaining why national capitalism
could not and has not been able to developed, that is to say, in
other words, why it is improper to speak of nation and national States in the Continent, especially in the nineteenth century.

It is important to underline that, as far as this point is concerned, and conversely to his conception of the nation, Samir
Arnin goes much further than Soler.

*"The peripheral bourgeoisie," the author points out, "do
not assume the functions of management and centralization
of the economies of the periphery [...] The weakness of the
bourgeoisie will thus mean **the absence of a bourgeois nation
and the non-national character of the local bourgeoisie".*[37]

Both authors agree, however, on a common point: in the
denial of nationalism as a bourgeois ideology.

*"The fact that the first national states exhibited a bour-
geois content because of the historical agent that promoted
their organization," notes Soler, "has led, however, to the il-
legitimate equation to be bourgeois and to also be national,
thus forgetting the varied range of mediations through which
nations have been constituted, and continue to be constituted,*

---

(36) V. I. Lenin, Ob. cit., pp. 36, 37, 40 y 41.

(37) Samir Amin, Ob., cit., p. 34. Cursivas de Samir Amin [Samir Amin Italics].

in contemporary and current history".[38] Samir Amin, on his behalf, points out that the existence of an integrated capitalist market as a requirement of the nation in Stalin's conception [...] "leads also to a political conclusion, which was, in its origin: that nationalism is a bourgeois ideology, and that the ideology of the proletariat should not have nationality. Here, as often as it is, Amin adds, Trotskyism is not different, since it is the twin brother of Stalinism, and both are legitimate children, although they are 'damn' of Leninism".[39]

This conclusion consistent with the authors' position results from misleading inference.

In this regard, here is what Lenin maintains:

"The principle of nationality is historically inevitable in bourgeois society, and in view of the existence of this society, the Marxist fully recognizes the historical legitimacy of the national movements, but for this recognition not to become an apology for nationalism, it is necessary to limit strictly and exclusively to the progressive elements of such movements, so that it does not contribute to muddy the consciousness of the proletariat with the bourgeois ideology. The awakening of the masses after feudal lethargy is progressive; it is progressive its struggle against all national oppression, its struggle for the sovereignty of the people, for national sovereignty[...] But beyond this limit the proletariat cannot support nationalism, for beyond that the 'positive' activity of the bourgeoisie begins in its eagerness to consolidate nationalism. To consecrate nationalism in a certain 'equitably limited' sphere, to 'constitute'

---

(38) Ricaurte Soler, *La nación hispanoamericana [The Spanish American Nation]*; Ediciones Instituto Nacional de Cultura [National Institute of the Culture Editions], Colección Cultural Pensamiento Nacional [National Cultural Thought Collection], pp. 73-74; Panamá, 1978.

(39) Samir Amin, Ob. cit., p. 30.

*nationalism, to raise solid and lasting barriers among all na-
tions by a particular form: such is the ideological basis and
content of national autonomy cultural. This idea is bourgeois
from end to end, and false from one end to another. The proletariat cannot lend its support to any consecration of nationalism; on the contrary, it supports everything that helps eliminate national distinctions and overturn national barriers, all
of which tighten the link between nationalities, all leading to
the fusion of nations. To act otherwise is to take sides with the
reactionary nationalist petty bourgeoisie".*[40]

3. SOME WRONG VARIANTS ABOUT THE NA-
TURE OF THE STATE IN LATIN AMERICA.

For some authors the Latin American state of the last third
of the nineteenth century and much of the twentieth century is
an oligarchic, national and dependent state.

*"The dependent national state" for example, Anibal Qui-
jano was referring to the Peruvian State "who crossed the
class problem with the national problem, in relation to the
hegemony of imperialist capital, would also assume, on new
bases, its oligarchical continuity. In other words, a national-dependent oligarchic state emerged, an oligarchic state
that was governed by the concrete model of political domination, but of a bourgeois social base, independent, conflicted,
but combined, national, by the formally independent condition
of the nation-state; dependent (the word is not very adequate),
because the hegemony of imperialist capital in the functions*

---

(40) V.I. Lenin, Ob. Cit., pp. 26-27 (Cursivas de JETA [JETA Italics])

of the state was clothed with the foreign provenance of the imperialist bourgeoisie". [41]

Octavio Ianni, José Luis Reyna and Manuel Villa share the same position.

"It seems convenient," says Ianni, "Quijano's argument, regarding the national-dependent and at the same time oligarchic character of the Peruvian state". [42] *"According to Quijano," Reyna and Villa add, "the Peruvian state is constituted as oligarchic, national and dependent. This schematic characterization; otherwise attributable to the Latin American state with its respective national variants, seems to be a point that requires no further discussion".* [43]

"It was the countries that, by the impulse of the world market, developed their agricultural sectors," says Arnaldo Córdova, "those who soon succeeded in establishing their national oligarchies[...] Not counting the ten years of the war of independence in Mexico, devastating and ruinous like no other in the continent, this country had to wait fifty-five years for the beginning of the constitution, **manu military** *of the na-*

---

(41) Anibal Quijano, *Imperialismo, clases sociales y Estado en el Perú: 1895-1930 [Imperialism, social classes and State in Peru: 1895-1930]*, en **Clases sociales y crisis política en América Latina (Seminario de Oaxaca)** organizado por el instituto de Investigaciones sociales de la UNAM [in **Social classes and political crisis in Latin America (Seminar of Oaxaca)** organized by the institute of Social Investigations of the UNAM], coordinado por [coordinated by] Baúl Benítez, Siglo XXI [21st Century], la. ed., p. 142, México, 1977.

(42) Octavio Ianni, *Clases subalternas y Estado oligárquico [Subaltern classes and oligarchic State]*, comentario a la ponencia de [comment to the paper of] Anibal Quijano, en 0b. cit., p. 158.

(43) José Luis Reyna y [and] Manuel Villa A. *Estructura y proceso en el análisis de la dominación en América Latina [Structure and process in the analysis of domination in Latin America]*, comentario a la ponencia de [comment to the paper of] Anibal Quijano, en Ibid., p. 201.

*tional oligarchic state, with the accession to power of General
Porfirio Diaz, ".*[44]

This position is clearly contradictory. The State cannot be **oligarchic** and [...] "to the extent that it guaranteed above all the interests of a foreign bourgeoisie"[45] **dependent**, and at the same time **national**. Even less, if [...] "in the coalition of political power, pre-capitalist classes were in the immediate predominant as the concrete social basis of the state".[46] "This was, in this sense," says Quijano, "a combination of bourgeois and manorial in its concrete appearance and in that appearance the lordly was predominant.

On the other hand [...] the very existence of this coalition of power, as well as the basic state function of guaranteeing the hegemony of imperialist capital, made that, in spite of that predominant manorial base, as well as through it, the state had in its essential function a predominant bourgeois character".[47]

A state with manorial pre-capitalist classes as the predominant and concrete social base, and with a basic state function of guaranteeing the hegemony of imperialist capital, cannot be at all a **National State**, in the terms in which it understands Marxism-Leninism. It is no coincidence; therefore, that Arnaldo Córdova maintains that in the period between the first two thirds of the nineteenth century, called by Porfirian ideologues, quite rightly, ([...]) as the 'period of anarchy', it contemplates a National state that it is only of name; without effective con-

---

(44) Arnaldo Córdova, *Los orígenes del Estado en América Latina [The origins of the State in Latin America]*, en la revista [in the magazine] **Cuadernos Políticos [Political Papers]**, México, octubre-diciembre de [October-December] 1977» p. 34 y 38.

(45) Anibal Quijano, Ob., cit., p. 140.

(46) Ibid., p. 141.

(47) Ibid., p. 141.

trol over the population and territory, without authority and content, by a look of local powers whose autonomy was the undoubted sign of the weakness of the central powers [...] "All this reminds us that the development process of our country, as in almost all underdeveloped countries, is essentially the opposite of what is observed in Western Europe, where the unifying function is developed by a national market that is organized outside the State, also national, and even, acting on the latter as a driving force".[48]

Certain authors who try to detach themselves from this conception fail to take the decisive step and, as a consequence, fall into continuous contradictions. Such is the case of Francisco Weffort.

[...] "The class of the great landowners" says this author, "although it has been able to organize national states, it has no conditions to formulate or to allow the historical realization of an ideal of nation unrelated to production for the external market".[49]

The contradiction is obvious: it cannot be argued that the class of the great landowners cannot formulate an ideal of nation unrelated to production for the external market, and at the same time affirm that this class has organized national states.

---

(48) Arnaldo Córdova, **La formación del poder político en México [The formation of political power in Mexico]**; Editorial ÉRA [ERA Editorial]. 2a. ed., pp. 9-10 México, 1972.

(49) Francisco C. Weffort, *Clases populares y desarrollo social [Popular classes and social development]*, en **Populismo, marginación y dependencia** [in **Popularism, marginalization and dependence**] (Ensayos de interpretación sociológica [Essays on sociological interpretation]); Editorial Universitaria Centro Americana EDUCA [Editorial University of Central America EDUCA, la. ed., p. 63; Costa Rica, 1973.

In an effort to recognize its contradiction, Weffort points out [...] "that the oligarchic state is only partially a state in the sense that European history has shaped this concept".[50]

"The process of formation of the state," he points out in developing this idea, "in European countries follows a different path. As is well known, they are essentially compatible with the process of forming an internal market (including the labor market), with An industrial bourgeoisie that assumes political hegemony and conforms the state in its own way and its interests [...] Thus, the State as a Nation State and an industrial bourgeoisie as a national bourgeoisie are formed jointly in countries which, at this stage, already assume a dominant position in relation to large sectors of the non-industrial world".[51]

Therefore, "when we refer to the national economy in the same way as the nation-state, we face from the beginning the paradox of its validity in original and constitutionally dependent countries. Hence the examination of the conditions of validity of liberalism leads us to examination of the more general problem of the validity of the Nation-State in dependent countries".[52]

This contradiction that Weffort himself emphasizes does nothing more than express, according to the author, an earlier paradox:

[...] "The strange composition between Traditional Oligarchy and Liberal State"[...].[53]. "For internal reasons as

---

(50) Ibid., p. 63.

(51) Ibid., p. 41-42.

(52) Ibid., p. 58.

(53) Ibid., p. 54-55.

well as for external reasons, it's noted that, the nation-state of a dependent country is condemned, at the stage called by the economists of 'outwards development', to take liberal forms on structures with oligarchic content".[54]

"Domination of agrarian elites and liberal ideology, oligarchic content and democratic forms, it is there where one of the roots of the Latin American state and one of the political peculiarities of dependent countries is".[55] *However, "the paradoxical condition of the Latin American states is not exhausted at the level of the relationships between liberalism and the oligarchy [...] These contradictory relationships only express a more fundamental paradox, which is that of the countries that although dependent on the level of economic relationship, nevertheless sought to manifest themselves autonomously, as a nation-state, at the political level".*[56]

These paragraphs reveal the author's confusion. We have already said on various occasions that between liberal and conservative there were no **antagonistic** economic contradictions. That is why the triumph of the liberals did not lead to the destruction of the economic base of the conservatives, but to an oligarchic state that was no more than the political expression of the fusion of these groups. Hence the liberal forms of the state over structures of oligarchic content were perfectly compatible. The strange composition is not, therefore, between traditional oligarchy and liberal state, but on the fact that these dependent countries according to the author, "nevertheless tried to manifest themselves with autonomy, as a **Nation-State**, at the political level".

---

(54) Ibid., p. 60.

(55) Ibid., p. 55

(56) Ibid., p. 62

Some Latin American scholars consider that in some countries of the region, particularly in Mexico, the system has begun to acquire, from the fifties, the features of a monopoly capitalism state. Therefore, the State has assumed the character of a state of monopoly capitalism.

"Conscious that historical facts can never be clearly and arbitrarily demarcated," Alonso Aguilar points out, "it could perhaps be tentatively suggested that Mexican capitalism began to become state monopoly capitalism in the late 1940s and beginning of the next decade".[57] "Unlike other times when the state and private monopoly capital operated quite independently of each other," he points out elsewhere, "in the last two decades they have greatly strengthened their relationships, arising from the internal dynamics and the contradictions themselves of the accumulation process, the Mexican variant of state monopoly capitalism".[58] "There is no doubt," Carrión points out, "that the changes are great in Mexican society since the 1920's and especially for a quarter of a century, when the country enters the phase of state monopoly capitalism".[59] "The issue," Boron says, "is of prime importance since the impressive development of the CME has altered the anatomy and functioning of the contemporary capitalist state, both in the 'advanced' and peripheral and de-

---

(57) Alonso Aguilar M., *La Oligarquía [The Oligarchy]*; en [in] Jorge Carrión y [and] Alonso Aguilar M., **La burguesía, la oligarquía y el Estado [The bourgeoisie, the oligarchy and the state]**, Ed. Nuestro Tiempo [Our Time Edition], la. ed., p. 170; México, 1972.

(58) Alonso Aguilar M., *Capitalismo monopolista de Estado, subdesarrollo y crisis [Monopoly capitalism of the State, underdevelopment and crisis]*, en revista **Estrategia** [in **Strategy** magazine] No. 10, p. 58, julio-agosto [July- August], 1976.

(59) Fernando Carmona, *México: capitalismo monopolista de Estado y estructura del proletariado [Monopoly capitalism of state and structure of the proletariat]*, en revista **Estrategia** [in **Strategy** magazine] No. 5, p., 53, septiembre-octubre [September-October], México, 1975.

pendent societies, which has begun to stimulate interest in the study of its most outstanding manifestations. In Latin America the CME expansion was more recent and is associated with both the adoption of key-case countercyclical policies and the requirements of the process of induced substitution industrialization in those countries that had already established a certain industrial base prior to the crisis, by the crash of 1929".[60] "The emergence of the CME" adds Semo, "inevitably represents a shift in the balance of power between the state and private monopoly capital, and a relative subordination of the former. The conflicts and frictions that will originate this process will be a very important aspect of Mexican reality in the coming decades".[61]

It was Enrique Semo who best presented the theoretical basis of this conception. Here is his argument.

"In the countries of late capitalist and dependent development," says this author, "monopolies make their appearance very soon. Capitalism and monopoly are united from the beginning. However, one thing is the existence of monopolies and another very different, the monopoly phase of capitalism. A country only reaches that stage of its development, when conditions have been created that make possible to transform the monopolies into the dominant sector of the system as a whole. In Mexico, the first major monopolies appear as early as the twentieth century. However, the monopoly phase was not achieved until the 1960s. "Lenin would say", Semo continued, "that if one wanted to stamp a synthetic definition of

---

(60) Atilio Borón, *Nuevas formas del Estado latinoamericano [New forms of the Latin America State]*, en **Cuadernos Políticos** [in **Political Notebooks**] No. 15, pp. 36—37, enero-marzo [January-March]; México, 1978.

(61) Enrique Semo, *Reflexiones sobre el capitalismo monopolista en México [Reflections on monopoly capitalism in Mexico]*, en la revista **Historia y Sociedad** [in the magazine **History and Society**] No. 17, p. 29, México, 1978.

*the imperialist phase, it could be said that **imperialism is the monopolistic state of capitalism**". "The paradoxes of history", he adds, "want a group of countries at the end of the twentieth century to reach the monopoly phase of development without becoming imperialists at the same time. That is, that these countries will have a monopoly bourgeoisie, and will pass through all the rigors of monopoly domination, but will continue to be dependents and importers of capital".*[62]

Well, this position seems to us obviously wrong, and with dire political consequences.

No underdeveloped country, by its very situation, could ever be in the phase of state monopoly capitalism, that is, at a stage where the state assumed the character of a state of monopoly capitalism. From this point of view, it's incomplete and therefore erroneous, Semo's assertion that "a country only reaches that stage of its development, when conditions have been created that make possible the transformation of monopolies into the dominant sector of the system considered as a whole", then the author loses sight of the fact that *"Capitalism was changed into capitalist imperialism **only** when it reached a certain, very **high** degree of its development, when some of the fundamental characteristics of capitalism began to become its antithesis, when the features of the transition period from capitalism to a higher economic and social structure took shape and manifested themselves across the line".*[63]

Therefore, in order for a country to reach the stage of state monopoly capitalism, it would be necessary for it to have

---

(62) Enrique Semo, Ob. cit., pp. 30-32. Negritas de Semo [Semo Bold].

(63) V.I. Lenin, *El Imperialismo, Fase Superior del Capitalismo [Imperialism, Higher Phase of Capitalism]*, en **Obras Escogidas** en tres tomos [in **Selected Works** in Three Volumes]; Editorial Progreso [Progress Editorial], p. 761, Moscú [Moscow], 1966 (Cursivas de JETA [JETA Italics]).

been transformed into an imperialist country with all that implies, i.e.: (1) the concentration of production and capital had reached a high degree of development, that monopolies play a decisive role in economic life; (2) financial capital and the financial oligarchy had emerged on the basis of the merger of bank capital with industrial capital; (3) the export of capital, unlike the exportation of goods, was particularly important; (4) international monopoly associations of capitalists had formed that would fight for the economic distribution of the world; And (5) these monopoly associations of capitalists demanded a new territorial division of the world.

Naturally, it would be illogical to argue that Mexico, or any other underdeveloped country, which has not even succeeded in consolidating a national state, is passing through such a phase; except at a time when some of these essential features of imperialism are historically unattainable.

For the same reason, it is equally illogical to conceive that by the "end of the twentieth century a group of countries will reach the monopoly stage without becoming at the same time imperialists"; that is to say, that these countries have a monopoly bourgeoisie "going through all the rigors of monopoly domination," and that they remain dependent and importers of capital.

4. WHY WAS THE UNITED STATES INDUSTRIALIZED IN THE NINETEENTH CENTURY WHILE ARGENTINA DID NOT ACHIEVE IT?

In light of the study of the specific social classes of underdevelopment and the nature of those of the States that emerged in Latin America through the process of independence, it is not difficult to solve one of the questions that many thinkers have raised in the case of Brazil and especially of Argentina.

For what reasons did the United States become industrialized in the nineteenth century, while Brazil, and especially Argentina, did not succeed, transforming the latter into the most advanced underdeveloped country in the early twentieth century?

In the case of Brazil, the limitations imposed on the Brazilian government in trade agreements with England from 1810 to 1827 appear to be, for some authors, the reason for this fact.

"This point of view," Furtado says, "common among scholars of the Brazilian economy, is set forth, for example, by R. Simonsen:[64] *"We had to adopt at that time a policy similar to that which the American nation continued in the period of their economic training. Producers of colonial goods, facing a world closed by 'colonial police' (Simonsen alluded to one of the disciples of the Portuguese version of the Treaty of Commerce of 1810, which translated* **policy** *for police) we became, nevertheless, champions of economic liberalism in America".*[65] *"The 'opening of the ports' decreed in 1808, Furtado noted, was the result of an imposition of events. Followed by the treaties of 1810 which transform England into privileged power, with rights of extraterritoriality and preferential tariffs at extremely low levels; these treaties will constitute, during the whole first half of the century, a serious limitation to the autonomy of the Brazilian government in the*

---

(64) Celso Furtado, **Formación Económica del Brasil [Economic Formation of Brazil]**; Fondo de Cultura Económica [Fund of Economic Culture], 2 edición en español [2nd edition in Spanish], p. 107-108, nota [note]; Río de Janeiro, 1974.

(65) R. Simonsen, *Historia económica do Brasil [Economic History of Brazil]*, 3 ed., p.406; (S. Pablo, 1957); citado por [cited by] Celso Furtado; Ob., cit., p. 108.

economic sector. The definitive separation of Portugal in 1822 and the agreement by which England succeeded in consolidating its position in 1827 are two other fundamental facts at that stage of great political events. Finally, it is possible to refer to the elimination of the personal power of Don Pedro I in 1831 and the consequent definitive ascension to the power of the dominant colonial class, formed by the gentlemen of the great agriculture of export.[66]

"However, there seems to be no basis, " Furtado reiterates, *"the common criticism made to these agreements, according to which they prevented the industrialization of Brazil at that stage, removing the instrument of protectionism from the hands of the government [...] The assumption that it would be within Brazil's reach, assuming that it had full freedom of action, to adopt a policy identical to that of the United States, at the early stage of the nineteenth century, does not stand up to a detailed analysis of the facts [...] Protectionism arose In the United States, as a general system of economic policy, at a very advanced stage of the nineteenth century, when the foundations of its economy had already consolidated. By the first American tariff of 1789, cotton fabrics had only a 5% tax and the average for all goods was 8.5%. Several readjustments allowed the tariff for cotton fabrics to reach 17.5% in 1808, at a time when the American textile industry could already be considered consolidated [...] At the time of its independence the American population was more or less equivalent in quantity to that of Brazil . The social differences, however, were profound, for while in Brazil the ruling class was the group of large slave farmers, in the United States a class of small farmers and a group of large urban merchants dominated the country [...] Condition basic for the development of the Brazilian economy in the first half of the nineteenth century, would have been the expansion of its exports. To foster indus-*

---

(66) Celso Furtado, Ob., cit., p. 101.

trialization at that time without the support of a capacity to import in expansion would be to try the impossible in a country lacking a technical base [...] Even leaving aside the consideration that an intelligent industrialization policy would be impracticable in a country run by a class of slave farmers, it is necessary to recognize that the first condition for the success of that policy would have been a firm and extensive expansion of the export sector. The main cause of the relative delay of the Brazilian economy in the first half of the nineteenth century was, therefore, the stagnation of its exports". [67]

Well, in the first half of the nineteenth century, in our opinion, there were no conditions in Brazil to promote a process of industrialization. And the fundamental reason of this fact is emphasized by Furtado himself.

[...] "An intelligent policy of industrialization ***would be impracticable in a country run by a class of great slave farmers"[...].*** [68]

This is the fundamental condition and reason sine-qua-non, which explains why Brazil evolved in the sense of becoming a vast underdeveloped region in the twentieth century. All other causes of the great delay of the Brazilian economy in that first half of the nineteenth century, as the "stagnation of its exports" pointed out by Furtado, or the absence of a **protectionist** policy identical to that of the United States, in that first period of the nineteenth century, aggravated by the limitations imposed on the Brazilian government in trade agreements with England from 1810 to 1827, that Simonsen maintains, the latter point of view so common among scholars of the Brazilian economy, become unnecessary.

---

(67) Ibid., pp.107-108.

(68) Ibid., pp. 113-114.

"Social differences," Furtado remarks, **"were profound, for while in Brazil the ruling class was the group of large slave farmers, in the United States a class of small farmers and a group of large urban merchants dominated the country"**.[69] See here how Furtado overlooks the class structure of the United States, at that time, the powerful cotton and slave oligarchy of the south which without it is impossible to understand the root, or rather, the terms of the problem.

In the case of Argentina, which in my opinion is the country that justifies the question, was the English historian Eric J. Hobsbawm who, in 1971, while we were talking at Birkbeck College of the University of London, **why if Argentina had better conditions than the United States during the nineteenth century could not be industrialized and the United States was able to.**

Certainly, when we compare Argentina in the first half of the nineteenth century with the United States, from the point of view of the specific social classes **of underdevelopment, Argentina had better conditions to promote an industrialization process than the United States. While it was true that in both countries a powerful modern, anti-national and foreign oligarchy had developed** *(the cattle exporters of the pampas Argentine, united with the great importers of the port of Buenos Aires, corresponded to the powerful slave oligarchy of the Cotton plantation of the South of the United States united to the great importers merchants).* **The great advantage in Argentina is that slavery never existed, while the cotton plantation was always based on slave labor with all that involved.**

The power of the southern cotton and slave planters was enormous.

---

(69) Ibid., p. 108.

"Cotton, which accounts for more than half the value of US exports," Furtado says, **"was the main dynamic factor in the development of the US economy in the first half of the nineteenth century. Its cultivation allowed the incorporation of abundant fertile lands in Alabama, Mississippi, Louisiana, Arkansas and Florida, which were used in a more or less identical way to what would happen in Brazil with coffee. Extensive forms of cultivation obliged us to always seek new lands and to penetrate the interior of the Continent. And mainly as a reflection of this expanding system in the south, the North American Midwest was populated, making room for the great currents of European colonization, which penetrated the center of the Continent by climbing the great rivers that linked them with the markets of the South [...] The industrial revolution, in the last quarter of the eighteenth century and in the first half of the nineteenth century, consisted mainly of a profound transformation of the textile industry [...] The first stage [...] clearly presents two basic characteristics: the mechanization of manufacturing processes of Textile industry and the substitution for the wool industry for the cotton, raw material whose production could be expanded more easily.** If England had the task of introducing the processes of mechanization, it was the United States that assumed the responsibility of the second stage: to provide the immense quantities of cotton which, in a few decades, enabled the physiognomy of the supply of textiles to be transformed throughout the world. Indeed, between 1780 and the mid-nineteenth century, the consumption of cotton by English factories increased from 2,000 tons to about 250,000". [70]

Contrary to what happened in the colonies of the large cotton plantations of the southern slave trade of the United States, exploited on the basis of slave labor in which consumption

---

(70) Celso Furtado, Ob., cit., pp.112, 111.

expenditures were concentrated in a small slave-owning aristocracy and satisfied with imports, in the colonies of small landowners in the north, largely self-sufficient, constituted communities with entirely different characteristics. In them the concentration of benefits was much lower and they were much less subject to abrupt economic contractions. As a consequence, the average consumption pattern was high relative to the *per capita* production level. On **the other hand, the abundance of land made European immigration attractive in the regime of temporary easement. When the possibility of regularly selling part of his agricultural production for the small owner, it became possible for him to finance the trip of an immigrant whose work would be exploited for four years. It is estimated that at least half of the European population that immigrated to the United States before 1700 was made up of people who had accepted one or another temporary easement regime.**[71]

It should be noted that colonies in the northern United States developed in the second half of the seventeenth and first half of the eighteenth century as an integral part of a larger system within which the dynamic element was constituted by the Caribbean regions producing tropical items; the penetration of sugar into the Caribbean islands forced out a substantial amount of the white population that was to settle in the northern colonies. These were, in particular, small owners who were forced to sell their land and transferred to these colonies with some capital. On the other hand, sugar disorganized and, in some places, eliminated subsistence agricultural production. The islands quickly became major importers of food, and the northern colonies, which had not yet known what to do with their surplus wheat production, were the main source of supply for the prosperous sugar colonies. Not only was the important trade flow that formed between

---

(71) Ibid., p. 38.

the two groups of English colonies left in the exportation of consumer goods. Without having hydraulic power to move the sugar mills, the islands depended primarily on draft animals as an energy source. They also did not have wood to manufacture the boxes in which sugar was exported. Both had to come from the north. This important commerce was carried out mainly in ships of the settlers of New England, which came to foment the shipbuilding in that region. This industry, finding exceptionally favorable conditions due to the abundance of suitable wood, developed intensely transforming itself into one of the main export activities of the northern colonies. Finally, mention should be made of the installation of an important industry derived from sugar cane: the distillation of alcoholic beverages. In this case the integration was carried out with the French Antilles. These, who were banned from using the raw material at their disposal, to avoid competition with the beverage industries of the Metropolis, were selling at extremely low prices. Northern settlers took advantage of these low prices to compete advantageously with the English West Indies in this highly profitable business.[72]

On the other hand, the restrictive measures with respect to the manufacturing production that England imposed on its colonies in the mercantilist era had to be applied very specially in the United States. The general lines of English policy were as follows: to promote in the colonies of the north those industries that did not compete with those of the Metropolis, allowing it to reduce its imports from other countries; Not to allow the manufacturing production of the same in the other sectors to compete with the industries of the Metropolis in other colonial markets. Coercive measures began to emerge when the colonies of the north come to compete with the Metropolis in exports of manufactures. In the special case of steel, there was concern to make it difficult to produce in the colony,

---

(72) Celso Furtado, Ob., cit., pp. 35-36

but in compensation the production of iron was encouraged to allow England to reduce its dependence on the Baltic countries. On the other hand, the colonies themselves, faced with difficulties in importing the manufactures they needed, from the outset created an awareness of the need to foster domestic production. Already in 1655 Massachusetts passed a law forcing all families to produce the tissues they needed. Many colonies prohibited the export of certain raw materials, such as leathers, to be manufactured locally. Finally, it is important to mention the extraordinary advance of the shipbuilding industry that would play a fundamental role in the development that occurred during the Napoleonic wars. Already before independence, three quarters of the American trade took place on its own ships. The war of independence that interrupted for several years the supply of English manufactures, created a strong stimulus for domestic production, which already had a basis for expansion. Almost immediately followed the beginning of the stage of great political upheavals in Europe, which stimulated the development of the American economy. For many years, the United States was the only neutral power that had a large merchant fleet. With the difficulties of European supply, the English and French West Indies were directed towards the North American food market. In order to have an idea of this prosperity, it is sufficient to note that from 1789 to 1810 the American fleet grew from 202,000 to 1,425,000 tons, and that all these ships were built in the country.[73]

A profound conflict arose between two completely different types of economy: the industrial and agrarian north with a free capitalist and abolitionist economy, mainly directed to the domestic market, and the southern slave trade with an economy of cotton export, slavery and importer of English manufactures.

---

(73) Celso Furtado, Ob., cit., pp. 109-110.

This antagonism reached its most serious political expression in early 1861. **Abraham Lincoln** lost a senatorial contest in which he demanded a halt to the expansion of **slavery,** but in **1860** he and **Douglas** again faced: this time as the presidential candidates Republican and Democrat. By then the tension between North and South was extreme. Douglas urged Southern Democrats to remain in the Union, but these in turn named their own presidential candidate (**John C. Breckinridge**) and threatened to separate if the Republicans were victorious. Most in the Southern and Border states voted against Lincoln, but the North supported him and won the election. In March **1861**, when Lincoln took office, **South Carolina, Mississippi, Florida, Alabama, Georgia, Louisiana**, and **Texas** were constituted in the **Confederate States of America** with **Jefferson Davis** as president, proclaiming his secession from the Union, act which Lincoln declared illegal in his inaugural address. This act marks the start of civil war or secession war. Lincoln's priority was to maintain the United States as one country. The first act of war was the confederate assault on the **Fort Sumter** garrison on April 12, 1861. The repression of the army upon the **recovery of Fort Sumter** caused the Confederate states to join **Virginia, Arkansas, Tennessee, and North Carolina**. Thus began the civil war between the Confederate States of the South and the States of the North, which would end the victory of the latter in 1865. With the culmination of the war the union is maintained and the antagonism between the two types of economics.[74]

The north, therefore, not only ended with the powerful **slave-owning oligarchy of the cotton plantation united to the great merchants importers of English manufacture,**

---

(74) Wikipedia (la enciclopedia libre [the free encyclopedia]), La Guerra de Secesión [The War of Secession] (artículo [article]). Fecha de consulta [Date of consultation]: 5 noviembre [November 5th] 2015. Disponible en [Available at]: https://es.wikipedia.org/wiki/Guerra_de_Secesión.

but applied a protectionist policy and allowed the industrialization of the whole country.

In Argentina the reverse happened. The powerful modern oligarchy, antinational and foreign of the port of Buenos Aires was the victorious one in the civil war that happened to the independence, and; the "type of economy," "style," or "outward expansion model," based on the production of primary products for large industrial centers and the importation of manufactured goods from those centers, was the type of economy that predominated in form Almost exclusive until the First World War.

[...] "The Buenos Aires bourgeoisie and the landlords of the neighboring fields, the two fundamental social classes of the Province-Metropolis," Abelardo Ramos stresses, "they assumed a role that the remaining Intendancies, now divided into Provinces, had not conferred on it. Buenos Aires broke up with Spain and intended to replace the King by itself in the hegemony with respect to the remaining provinces. "All the history of later Argentina," adds the author "is the history of imposing that hegemony and the account of the struggle of the provinces to reject it. The Argentine civil wars are based on this pretense and on the refusal of the Buenosairean interests, either with Rivadavia and Miter, as men of the pro-British commercial bourgeoisie, or Rosas, as representative of the landlords, to accept the equality of Buenos Aires with the interior provinces, to organize the Nation in the vice-regal limits and to divide the customs rents between all its parts. It is true that the 'Nation' had been expressed until that moment by a power external to Hispanic America itself, that is, by The Spanish monarchy. When leaving this link, Buenos Aires is obsessed by the exclusive enjoyment of its income and loses sight of the whole of the Spanish-Catholic unity. His condition will be celebrated and

from the first years of the revolution he cherished the idea, seldom clearly manifested, of his complete independence from the rest of the Spanish-American territory of which he was a part of".[75]

"If the Coast," says Milciades Peña, "coincided with Buenos Aires in its free exchange of livestock opposed to the protectionism of the interior of the interior, its interests were united with those of the interior and were in direct opposition to those of Buenos Aires before the decisive problem of Almost everything that the country exported and imported went through the Customs of the port of Buenos Aires, and Buenos Aires was the one who stayed with the juicy produce of that Customs, without giving the other provinces no share in its profits".[76]

The farmers of Buenos Aires, on the other hand, tried to convert their own port in the unique national port of the Coast. This monopoly of customs and the port contrary to national unity, favored all the centrifugal tendencies in the regions of the Coast that had superior ports and in better capacity to give direct output to their exports.[77]

---

(75) Jorge Abelardo Ramos, **Historia de la Nación latinoamericana [History of the Latin America Nation]**; A. Peña Lillo editor, pp. 246-247, Buenos Aires, Argentina, 1968.

(76) Milciades Peña, **El paraíso terrateniente [The Landlords Paradise] (Federales y Unitarios, forjando la civilización del cuero [Federal and Unitarian, forging the civilization of leather])**; Ediciones Fichas [Fichas' Edition], 2ª. Ed., p. 22; Buenos Aires, 1972.

(77) "Los conflictos entre Rosas y Francia -apunta Giberti-, y en menor medida Inglaterra, tuvieron una repercusión favorable sobre el Litoral. Los estancieros, principalmente los de Entre Ríos, ampliaron enormemente sus negocios gracias al comercio directo -sin intermediación porteña- con los países europeos. Los barcos de ultramar entraban por el Paraná y el Uruguay trayendo manufacturas y llevando los cueros, tasajo, astas, cerdas, tabaco y yerba que antes sólo podían salir por Buenos Aires. Pero en 1849 cuando Rosas llega a un acuerdo con Inglaterra, por el cual aquella reconoce el monopolio portuario de Buenos

Finally, Buenos Aires' free trade policy prevented part of the expansion of Coastal demand from being channeled towards the purchase of goods in the rest of the country. The interior could have indirectly received the benefits of this expansion of exports through the increase of its own sales to satisfy the growing demand of the Coast. However, the freedom of imports followed by Buenos Aires drowned this feasibility and, with it, any possibility of diffusing the dynamic impulses generated by the expansion of the Coastal exports. But, in addition, the products imported in Buenos Aires and distributed from there to the Mediterranean provinces competed with the local production within each region and affected the traditional currents of the interchange of the interior regions with each other. "The figures available on imports made by the port of Buenos Aires reveal that around the mid-nineteenth century about 50% of total imports consisted of textiles, beverages, sugar, mate and tobacco, all of which directly competed with the Many of these items, particularly textiles, had a degree of refinement and a level of prices against which the precarious and inefficient crafts of the rest of the country could not com-

---

Aires comprometiéndose a no navegar los ríos interiores, el Litoral ve cerrarse la fuente de su prosperidad. Las naves debían recalar en Buenos Aires para descargar y cargar, y nuevamente los productores del Litoral debieron rendir tributo a la aduana bonaerense [The conflicts between Rosas and France," Giberti notes, "and to a lesser extent England, had a favorable impact on the Coast. The farmers, mainly those of Entre Ríos, greatly expanded their businesses thanks to the direct trade "without Buenosairean intermediation" with the European countries. The overseas ships entered the Paraná and Uruguay, bringing in manufactures and carrying the leathers, tasajo, antlers, sows, tobacco and yerba that before could only leave through Buenos Aires. But in 1849 when Rosas arrived at an agreement with England, by which it recognizes the port monopoly of Buenos Aires committing itself to not navigate the interior rivers, the Coast is closing the source of its prosperity. The ships had to be stationed in Buenos Aires to unload and load, and again the producers of the Coast had to pay tribute to the Buenosairean custom]". (Horacio Gilberti, **Historia económica de la ganadería [Economic history of livestock]**, Ed. Raigal, p. 132, Buenos Aires, 1954.

pete".[78] The provinces understood very well that the solution of their economic problems did not depend basically on them but of the Province of Buenos Aires. The civil war that overshadows the entire process of economic and political development of the country from independence until the second half of the nineteenth century is the unquestionable testimony of its lucidity.

That is, therefore, why Argentina, despite having better socio-economic conditions than the United States during the nineteenth century, failed to transform itself into an industrialized country.

---

(78) Aldo Ferrer, La **economía argentina** [The **Argentine economy**] **(las etapas de su desarrollo y problemas actuales [The stages of its development and current problems])**; Fondo de Cultura Económica [Fund of Economic Culture], 3a. ed., p. 82, Buenos Aires, 1968. Para este autor el período de transición en las etapas - del desarrollo de la economía argentina, abarca desde fines del siglo XVIII hasta 1860 [For this author the period of transition in the stages - of the development of the Argentine economy, it covers from the end of the eighteen century until 1860].